SINCE AFRICA

Mia McCullough

I0139626

BROADWAY PLAY PUBLISHING INC
224 E 62nd St, NY, NY 10065
www.broadwayplaypub.com
info@broadwayplaypub.com

SINCE AFRICA
© Copyright 2014 by Mia McCullough

First printing: February 2014
Second printing: April 2014
I S B N: 978-0-88145-587-8

Book design: Marie Donovan
Page make-up: Adobe Indesign
Typeface: Palatino
Printed and bound in the U S A

SINCE AFRICA was commissioned by the Cincinnati Shakespeare Festival and was also developed in part through Chicago Dramatists and The Playwrights Collective.

SINCE AFRICA was originally produced by Chicago Dramatists (Russ Tutterow, Artistic Director; Brian Loevner, Managing Director) opening on 18 March 2005. The cast and creative contributors were:

DIANE MACINTYRE................................. Morgan McCabe
ATER DHAL .... Abu Ansari
EVE MACINTYRE .... Anna Carini
DEACON REGGIE HUDSON .... Michael Edgar Myers

Director .... Russ Tutterow
Stage manager .... Domenick Danza
Scenic design .... Susan Kaip
Costume design .... Tiffany Trent
Sound design .... Barry Bennett
Lighting design .... Jeff Pines

SINCE AFRICA was first produced in New York by Red Fern Theatre Company (Melanie Moyer Williams, Executive Artistic Director; Ken Hall, Managing Director) at the Theatre at the 14th Street Y, opening on 22 February 2014. The cast and creative contributors were:

THE NAMELESS ONE............................Kristin D Carpenter
DIANE MACINTYRE..............................Jennifer Dorr White
ATER DHAL ....Matthew Murumba
EVE MACINTYRE ....Jenny Vallancourt
DEACON REGGIE HUDSON............................. Elton Beckett

Director... Nancy Robillard
Stage manager...Sammee Wortham
Percussionist..Evan Goldhahn
Scenic design...Robert Monaco
Costume design..Sarah J Holden
Properties design... Deb Gaouette
Lighting design .... Sam Gordon
Sound design.. Ian Wehrle
Assistant stage managers ....Jean Marie Hufford &
Jennifer Toth

CHARACTERS & SETTING

DIANE MACINTYRE, *a woman in her late 40s, early 50s; well-put-together, red hair*

REGGIE HUDSON, *a deacon at the local Catholic parish. 40s to 50s, light-skinned, African American*

EVE MACINTRYE, DIANE'S *daughter, 21*

ATER DHAL*, *(Pronounced "ah-TAIR") A southern Sudanese refugee—a Dinka, early 20s, tall and very dark-skinned.*

NAMELESS ONE, *an old spirit, played by girl/woman, black, or of mixed race, with her skin powdered to a ghostly alabaster. A dancing, non-speaking role.*

*As a matter of respect, ATER does not hold eye contact for very long with his elders. He has symmetrical scars on his forehead from a Dinka ceremony called "parapuol".

The victim of unfathomable tragedy and hardships, Ater has long since stopped showing overt signs of sadness and anger. His negative emotions are kept buried deep inside; and when he relates his history, it is with a matter-of-factness, a sparseness, that is startling. Only in Scenes 13 & 15, when he is dealing with a new crisis, does he unleash some of his emotions.

Notes on the NAMELESS ONE:

In order to make the NAMELESS ONE *as integral to the fabric
of the play as possible, it works best when staging to have
the* NAMELESS ONE *on stage all the time and then take her
away in spots where she feels inappropriate or distracting.
I originally pictured the* NAMELESS ONE *being played by a
girl 9-12 years old, but I have not found a girl who has the
groundedness, power and serenity to play such an old spirit.*

Time: 2001

Place: Chicago, Illinois

*The living room and kitchenette of a tiny one bedroom
apartment*

A car

*A psychologist's office: a comfy chair with a small table,
lamp & box of tissues*

A pulpit in a Catholic church

The foyer/entryway of the MACINTYRE *home*

PRONUNCIATIONS

Kakuma: kah-KOO-ma (Diane, Reggie, Eve) KAH-koo-ma (Ater)

Unga: un-GALL

Abuk: ah-BOUK

Dr Mazur: MAY-zer

Re: Scene 14

If it is possible to consult someone on the correct pronunciation of the lines in Dinka, then that would be ideal. If there are no local resources for this, it is better to do the scene in English than to butcher the Dinka language.

SOME NOTES ON MY PUNCTUATION

a dash— at the end of the line means the next line is cutting off this line. A dash— internally in a character's dialogue means they're cutting themself off; stopping short and rephrasing.

An ellipsis…. is a trailing off of a line.

If there is a /slash mid-sentence and a corresponding one in the next line of dialogue, this indicates where lines should overlap.

A paragraph break in the dialogue indicates a shift in tone or intent, but not a beat or a pause.

Special thanks to
Alephonsion Awer Deng
Malual Awak
and
Mathiang Deng

ACT ONE

Prelude

(African drums swell. The NAMELESS ONE *enters dancing with a Dinka spear and shield. After a few moment* DIANE *enters and the* NAMELESS ONE *stops dancing.* DIANE *spies the shield and spear, looks at them closely, takes them from the* NAMELESS ONE, *presses several bills into her hand and continues on her way. The* NAMELESS ONE *looks at the money, thoroughly perplexed.)*

(As lights shift, ATER *enters his apartment looking woozy. He lies down on the sofa.* DIANE *walks into the foyer of her home and hangs the shield on the wall next to the other African artifacts. The* NAMELESS ONE *follows her, watching, confused, intrigued.* DIANE *has the vague sense of another in the room, though she cannot see the* NAMELESS ONE. ATER *moans and the* NAMELESS ONE *rushes to him, touching his forehead, which he does not appear to feel. The* NAMELESS ONE *watches* DIANE *with curiosity as she cross to the chair in the psychologist's office.)*

Scene 1

(DIANE sits in the chair from a psychologist's office, a small table beside it, a box of tissues atop it. DIANE speaks to her shrink who is somewhere beyond the fourth wall. The Psychologist's voice is represented by a low African drum.)

DIANE: Well, it's small, you know, compared to the house. But it doesn't feel empty that way. I feel more contained now. Denise came in.

(Four drum beats)

DIANE: *(Good-natured scolding)* She's my decorator. I've told you that. *(Beat)* We kept some things. She was very patient. I changed my mind a lot. About which furniture. Which pieces…. I got a new bed.
I needed something I wouldn't feel lost in, you know? I need to feel the edges of…know where things end.
I've never slept alone before, can you believe that? I went from my parents' house to the sorority house to my husband's house.

(Soft drumming)

DIANE: I can't say it's been easy. I could use a prescription for sleeping pills, if you really want to know.

(Lights change.)

Interlude

(EVE enters, her winter coat and scarf on, car keys in her hands. She pulls on gloves. The NAMELESS ONE emerges and scopes out EVE, curious. She is suddenly taken by a spot on EVE's upper arm, slightly concerned. She pulls a long red silk magician's scarf from an unseen hole in the coat's sleeve.

EVE *touches her hand to her arm, sensing something, but unsure what. The* NAMELESS ONE *dances with the scarf, twirling it around* DIANE *as she enters in her coat. The* NAMELESS ONE *wraps the scarf around* DIANE'*s neck as she gets in the car with* EVE. *Lights shift to:)*

Scene 2

(DIANE *and* EVE *sit in the car.* EVE *is driving.)*

DIANE: ...first they fled to Ethiopia, then to Kenya—

EVE: Yeah, Mom, I know about them.

DIANE: You do?

EVE: Yeah. I do read, you know.

DIANE: I know you do. I just never think of us reading the same things.

EVE: You mean you forgot that I'm an adult, that I might actually read the newspaper, be aware of suffering in the world.

DIANE: Anyhow, that's where he's from.

EVE: So, what are you supposed to do? Show him around town, introduce him to your friends?

DIANE: Don't be so glib. I'll be showing him how to live here. Traffic rules, cultural etiquette, simple business transactions. Your basic survival skills.

(EVE *is shaking her head with a smirk.)*

DIANE: What? It's nothing I didn't teach you once upon a time.

EVE: It's just a little comical that you think you're going to teach survival skills to someone who probably trekked hundreds of miles, barefoot, through the African wilderness, in the middle of a civil war, twice, by the time he was eight years old.

DIANE: Whatever you want to call it, I'll be helping him adapt to his new surroundings.
Watch out for the—

EVE: DON'T tell me how to drive.
Please.
(Pause)
I don't know why you couldn't take the el. After all that going on about how independent you are in your new apartment.

DIANE: I just wanted a lift the first time. I didn't want to get lost and be late.

EVE: Uh huh.

DIANE: Thank you for driving me.

EVE: So, how old is this guy?

DIANE: I think he's about twenty-one. Something like that.

EVE: So, he's not a boy, at all.

DIANE: It's just what they call them. The Lost Boys.

(A tension filled silence. DIANE searches for something to say.)

DIANE: So your professors, they've been considerate about papers and things?

EVE: Yeah. Most of them are letting me turn things in by mid-February.

DIANE: Won't that make next semester overly busy for you?

(Three beats)

EVE: I think I want to take next semester off.

DIANE: Really. Isn't that the sort of thing you should consult me on?

EVE: I think that's what I'm doing. Right now.

DIANE: Oh.

EVE: It's just…I don't want to finish college like this. With this…coloring everything. I want some time to get my head together, you know?

DIANE: So when are you going to finish?

EVE: In the summer, if they'll let me.

DIANE: How will that affect your applications for graduate school?

(EVE *does a double-take, trying to read* DIANE.)

EVE: Dad didn't tell you?

(*Beat*)

DIANE: Apparently not.

(*Beat*)

EVE: I've applied for some internships with botanists doing research in South America. You know, I wouldn't get paid much, but the field experience…. Dad was the one who suggested it, actually. And it would be so great to get away from…

DIANE: Me?

EVE: Everything.

DIANE: Which countries in South America?

EVE: Brazil, Panama, Ecuador.

DIANE: Don't they abduct Americans in those places?

EVE: Americans are abducted in Africa, and it hasn't kept you from going.

DIANE: We have always been very careful.

EVE: Yeah, well, maybe I don't want the protected, sanitized, sterile version of everything. Maybe I want to actually see the place I'm going to.

DIANE: You didn't enjoy the trip to South Africa?

EVE: I did, Mom, but I was fifteen. I was a little young to realize that what I was seeing was what the South African tourism department wanted me to see, and not a reflection of that country's reality. I mean, Christ, we didn't even see anything outside the game park.

DIANE: So things aren't real until you put yourself in danger?

EVE: Mom, have we not learned that bad things can happen regardless of the precautions you take?

DIANE: Don't change the subject.

EVE: Have you heard from the airline?

DIANE: No.

EVE: Do you call them every day?

DIANE: Nearly.

EVE: You should call every day.

DIANE: They put me on hold for half an hour every time I call. It's quite a time commitment.

EVE: You have better things to do?

DIANE: I do have obligations. We're ramping up for the gala at the museum and I'm sure this Sudanese boy will take up some time. I'll be happy to give you the number so that you can call, if you feel that I'm not doing an adequate job.

EVE: I just don't understand why you would check him. I mean, how do someone's ashes not qualify as a carry-on item?

DIANE: How was I to know the airline would lose it? They were giving me an impossible time about repatriating his remains. I thought it would be safest to have the ashes locked in my trunk.

(Pause)

So will you be going back to Ann Arbor for this semester off or will you stay here?

EVE: I thought I'd stay here. Help you go through Dad's things.

DIANE: I'll set up a room for you in my apartment, then, if you'd like.

EVE: No. I am not moving in to Diane's Denial Den.

DIANE: I'm not comfortable with you staying in the house alone. It's not safe.

EVE: Of course it is. There are two alarm systems.

(Pause)

DIANE: You do realize I'm selling the house as soon as the market kicks in in the spring.

(EVE seethes.)

DIANE: Yes?

EVE: You're going to regret this. You're just freaking out because he's gone and the house feels empty.

DIANE: The house is empty.

EVE: No, it's not. It's full of my life, your life, your marriage, how can you sell that? So quickly, like it doesn't even matter.

DIANE: Of course /it matters.

EVE: /Why? So you don't have to face it?

DIANE: Eve. It's over. My life in that house is over. Your father is gone, you're going to graduate— hopefully—and I am going to have to move forward... somehow. I cannot live in the past, and you cannot expect me to.

EVE: How about the present, Mom? How 'bout taking a moment to acknowledge Dad's absence.

DIANE: Perhaps you and I have different /ways of—

EVE: / And what about the statue. What are you doing about her?

DIANE: I— Well— She's part of the property, she belongs to the house.

EVE: We all belong to the house.

DIANE: *(Noticing her surroundings)* This isn't a very nice neighborhood.

EVE: Well, they're not going to resettle refugees on the Gold Coast, Mom.

DIANE: This is where he lives?

(EVE is looking at addresses.)

EVE: Yeah, somewhere around here.

DIANE: I think we should lock the doors.

EVE: We don't need to lock the doors.

DIANE: Would you just do it?

EVE: Mom, you're about to get out and walk around, there is no point in locking the doors.

DIANE: Just do it, please.

(EVE locks the doors, giving up.)

DIANE: People are looking at us.

EVE: That's because we're driving a Mercedes with tinted windows very slowly down the street. They probably think we're drug dealers.

DIANE: What?

EVE: Okay, here we are.

DIANE: Where?

EVE: That place, right there.

(DIANE peers out the window at the building.)

DIANE: Will you come in with me?

EVE: Christ, Mom.

(Lights go to black.)

Scene 3

(Lights up on the front two rooms of an empty apartment. There is a sofa, a coffee table, an old arm chair, and a small kitchenette. There is an intercom on the wall next to the front door. A doorway leads to a bedroom and a bathroom. African drums thrum quietly in the background as the NAMELESS ONE checks out the apartment, turning the faucet on and off, at first with trepidation and then with glee. The flush of a toilet can be heard off stage. A groan. The NAMELESS ONE looks concerned. The door buzzer sounds and the NAMELESS ONE freezes.)

ATER: *(Off stage)* Oh… No no no.

(After a moment, ATER enters, doubled over. He runs to the intercom. It buzzes again.)

ATER: Yes. Okay. Hello. No. Which button… Talk. Yes, hello? …Listen.

(He pushes a different button.)

DIANE: *(Over intercom)* —is Diane. The volunteer. We spoke yesterday.

ATER: Yes, yes. Come up.

(ATER pushes another button, then dashes off to the bathroom, slamming the door shut. The NAMELESS ONE approaches the intercom, slowly. After several seconds there is a knock at the door. The NAMELESS ONE backs away.)

ATER: *(Off stage)* Ohhhhh. A minute. Please.

(A louder knock)

DIANE: *(Off stage)* Hello?

ATER: *(Off stage)* Wait. A minute. Please.

DIANE: Hello? Arthur? Are you in there?

(*The doorknob jiggles and the door opens a crack.*)

EVE: Mom! What are you doing?

DIANE: It's not locked.

EVE: You can't just waltz into someone's apartment.

DIANE: He buzzed us in.

EVE: Are you sure this is the right—Mom!

(DIANE *peeks into the apartment.*)

DIANE: Arthur? Are you here?

ATER: (*Off stage*) Yes. I'm sorry. I'm in the water closet. I am not feeling well.

(ATER *is in obvious discomfort.* EVE *mouthes the words "Water Closet" at her mother.*)

DIANE: Oh… Do you need to go to the doctor?

ATER: (*Off stage*) No. The others, in my group, they said it would stop.

DIANE: Did you get the flu?

ATER: (*Off stage*) No, it is from the food. It hurts my stomach. They say I will…adjust.

(EVE *is looking around.*)

EVE: This place is so small.

DIANE: Is no one else here?

ATER: (*Off stage*) They are at their jobs.

EVE: How many of them live here?

DIANE: Should I come back later?

ATER: (*Off stage*) Maybe that would be…ohhhhhhh.

DIANE: Oh, you poor boy. Do you have any tea? (*She goes into the kitchenette and begins looking through the cupboards.*)

EVE: *(Under her breath)* Oh, Christ.

ATER: *(Off stage)* What?

DIANE: Tea! Oh here's some. *(She looks for a kettle. Not finding one, she fills a pot with water and puts it on the stove.)*

ATER: *(Off stage)* What are you doing?

DIANE: I'm making you some tea.

ATER: *(Off stage)* Oh, no! You are my guest. You should not. I'm sorry.

DIANE: Don't apologize. I've got it taken care of. *(She pulls out a coffee cup and puts a tea bag in it.)*

EVE: *(Whispering)* Mom, you're upsetting him.

DIANE: *(Also whispering)* Just come in and close the door!

ATER: Did you say something?

DIANE: What did you eat?

ATER: *(Off stage)* Many things I do not know the name of. Yesterday, people from the church, they took us to a very loud place where basketball is played.

(DIANE looks at EVE, perplexed.)

EVE: *(To ATER)* The United Center?

ATER: *(Off stage)* Yes. Tell me, do you know of hot dogs?

DIANE: Hot dogs? Yes.

ATER: *(Off stage)* They are not made from dog?

DIANE: Dog? No. Cows or pig, usually, though it's hard to say what part.

(The toilet flushes again. The faucet can be heard. DIANE checks on the boiling water.)

(ATER emerges from the bathroom looking much better.)

ATER: Okay. I am here.

DIANE: Hello. I'm Diane MacIntyre. This is my daughter, Eve.

ATER: *(Shaking her hand)* Hello. I am Ater Dhal.

DIANE: Ater.

ATER: Yes.

DIANE: They told me Arthur. I'm sorry.

ATER: Yes, there has been confusion. Hello.

(ATER shakes EVE's hand.)

EVE: Nice to meet you.

ATER: Yes.

DIANE: Yes, it's very nice to meet you, Ater. …Welcome. To America.

(EVE is quietly mortified.)

ATER: Thank you. Why do they call it "hot dog" if it is not made of dog?

DIANE: I'm not sure. You should sit down. I'll pour you some tea.

ATER: Oh, you should not do this. You should sit and I should make the tea. It is my home, you are my guest.

EVE: Mom, maybe—

DIANE: Ater, it's all right. Sit down. You're not feeling well.

ATER: They told me it is rude to expect women to wait on you in America.

DIANE: Yes, well, when you're sick, you ought to have someone to make you some tea. Here, it's peppermint. It should settle your stomach.

ATER: Thank you. My brothers, they say everything will make me sick for a time. Until my stomach learns the new food.

EVE: How long does that take?

ATER: Several weeks, they say.

DIANE: What about the food in the cabinets? Can't you eat any of that?

ATER: I do not know how to get at much of it. And some of it, I don't know how to eat. Do I cook, do I mix with other food? I think this is why they send you to me.

EVE: What does that mean, you don't know how to "get at it"?

ATER: The tins. Someone showed us how to open them, the other volunteer, but we cannot get it to work. Here. This thing. Can you work it?

(ATER *goes to a kitchen drawer and pulls out an ancient, rusty can opener.* DIANE *takes it.*)

DIANE: Jesus, this thing must be fifty years old. And it's rusty. You shouldn't open anything with this.

ATER: So you do not know how to work it?

DIANE: I haven't the slightest. We'll just put that on the list of things to do. Buy a new can opener. And show you how to use it. What have you got in here? (*Looking in the cupboard*) Crackers, spaghettios, cake mix? Cranberry sauce? Water chestnuts? Who bought all this?

ATER: I don't know. I think it came from the church.

DIANE: What did you eat at the refugee camp?

ATER: Mostly lentils, and unga. Porridge we made with maize flour.

EVE: That's all?

ATER: Mostly.

DIANE: Well, no wonder you're sick, you've probably never ingested a simple carbohydrate in your life.

ATER: Excuse me, again.

(ATER *dashes off to the bathroom.* DIANE *and* EVE *look at one another at a loss.*)

EVE: You know what? I'm gonna go now.

DIANE: No, Eve—

EVE: Just turn left twice and you'll see the el, okay?

DIANE: Stay a few minutes longer.

EVE: Mom, you're doing fine. You've already taken over the kitchen.

(*Before* DIANE *can respond, the buzzer sounds. Both women freeze.*)

DIANE: Are you expecting someone else?

ATER: (*Off stage*) Maybe.

(*After a moment of debating,* DIANE *goes over to the intercom, takes a moment to inspect it, then pushes a button.*)

DIANE: Hello?

(*There is no response.*)

EVE: Mom, you have to push the—

DIANE: Oh, I see. Hello?

EVE: No, you have to hold it down.

(*There is a knock at the door. They freeze for a moment, unsure of what to do.* DIANE *looks back toward the bathroom,* EVE *moves to open the door.*)

DIANE: I should get it.

EVE: Okay.

(DIANE *opens the door to find* DEACON REGGIE HUDSON *wearing an inexpensive, but nice enough suit with an overcoat over it.*)

DIANE: Hello?

REGGIE: Hello. Mrs MacIntyre?

DIANE: *(Trying not to be alarmed)* Yes?

REGGIE: I'm Deacon Hudson. From Saint Bartholomew's?

DIANE: Oh, Deacon Hudson. I didn't realize you were...coming. Here. Today.

REGGIE: Didn't I mention it when we spoke?

DIANE: No.
I don't remember, honestly. Maybe you did.

REGGIE: May I come in?

DIANE: Of course. I'm sorry. This is my daughter, Eve.

REGGIE: Oh. Hello.

EVE: Hi.

DIANE: She came—

EVE: I was just leaving.

REGGIE: Don't leave on my account. I'm just dropping in to introduce myself. I like to meet my new volunteers. Especially if I won't have an opportunity to see them at mass. And I haven't had a chance to meet Arthur yet, either.

(The women exchange a glance. DIANE *is mildly indignant,* EVE *merely embarrassed for him.)*

EVE: His name is Ater.

REGGIE: Excuse me?

DIANE: It's not Arthur, it's Ater.

REGGIE: Oh. Really? Someone probably transposed it incorrectly. *(Beat)* Is he here?

DIANE: He's…he's indisposed, at the moment, he's not feeling well. Did your church donate this food?

REGGIE: I'm sure some of it came from us.

(The sound of flushing)

DIANE: Because it's making him sick. Making all of them sick./

EVE: /Mom/…

DIANE: /I mean, look. Some of it's ridiculous. There must be eight cans of cranberry sauce in here. It's full and it's generous, but with a donated can opener from the Bronze Age, it can hardly be called practical.

(ATER enters wiping his hands.)

ATER: Hello. I am Ater.

REGGIE: Hello. Deacon Hudson. Reggie Hudson.

(ATER and REGGIE shake hands.)

ATER: Oh, yes, from Saint Bartholomew's. My brothers say you are very nice.

REGGIE: Well, good.

DIANE: Ater, maybe since you're not feeling well, we should try this again tomorrow.

ATER: Okay. I am sorry.

DIANE: Don't be silly. You just take care of yourself. Drink your tea. Maybe eat some crackers. I set some on the counter over there.

ATER: Thank you.

DIANE: I'll see you tomorrow then. Should I come by in the morning? Around ten?

ATER: That would be good. Thank you.

EVE: It was nice to meet you, Ater.

ATER: Yes.

DIANE: And it was good to meet you, Deacon Hudson.

REGGIE: Yes. Likewise.

EVE: Bye.

(EVE *steps into the hall and* DIANE *follows.* DIANE *almost closes the door before she steps in again.*)

DIANE: And you really should lock this door. It's not safe to leave it open like this.

(DIANE *goes.* REGGIE *chuckles.*)

ATER: Did she make a joke?

REGGIE: No. Not really. …You probably should lock the door.

ATER: But if I do this, then Abraham, Joseph and Deng…they cannot come in.

REGGIE: They have keys, don't they?

ATER: Yes, in the bedroom, do you want to see them?

REGGIE: Uh, no. Maybe we could… We'll keep it unlocked for now.

ATER: Will you have some tea with me?

REGGIE: All right.

(ATER *gets another cup for him and pours some tea.*)

REGGIE: Your English is very good.

ATER: Thank you. They teach us in the camp.

REGGIE: Kakuma.

ATER: Yes.
And we shall have some of these, since Diane said so. Crackers.

(ATER *brings the mug of tea and the box of crackers over to the sofa, offering the tea to* REGGIE.)

REGGIE: Thank you.

(ATER *opens the box but does not know what to do with the sealed package inside.*)

ATER: Now how do I open?

REGGIE: Here, I'll show you.

(REGGIE *opens the package and offers* ATER *a cracker.* ATER *takes one and sits.*)

ATER: Thank you. You are not having some?

REGGIE: No, that's all right.

(ATER *sets down his cracker.*)

REGGIE: So, uh, how long have you been here? Four days?

ATER: Yes.

REGGIE: How was your trip? Over here.

ATER: Oh, very long. Many flights. Many airports.

REGGIE: I guess this was your first time in a plane.

ATER: Yes. I did not believe that something so big could leave the ground.

REGGIE: Yes. They're a leap of faith, airplanes. My wife and I have always wanted to go to Africa, but I have to admit I'm a little afraid of flying over the ocean.

ATER: Why do you want to go to Africa?

REGGIE: To see the motherland. To see where our ancestors came from. Before they were brought here as slaves.

ATER: Most of the women and girls in our village were taken as slaves, by the Arab traitors.

REGGIE: Yes, I, uh…read about that.

ATER: Do you know which country your people are from?

REGGIE: No… Probably one of the western countries.

There's this test they do now. They say they can tell you what part of Africa, what tribe, you're descended from. They get a sample of your cells, a tissue sample and they test it, your D N A. I don't really understand how it works—and then they say they can tell where you're from.

ATER: You are finding out, then?

REGGIE: I'm not sure when we'll get the results. I think it takes a while. I don't really know that much about it, to tell you the truth. It was Lorraine's idea. My wife's. She sent away for all of it without even telling me. I came home one day and she was chasing after me with this little scraping stick.
It's not the sort of thing I would do on my own.

ATER: It doesn't matter to you, where your people are from?

REGGIE: I guess I'm a little skeptical, that's all. I'm not a man of science—I'm not convinced they can really figure it out.

ATER: So when they tell you, you will not believe them.

REGGIE: I don't know. I wonder if it's a scam. A way to make money of off people's need to belong to something. They warn you, the people who run the test, that sometimes your heritage is so mixed that they can't isolate one tribe. Or you find out you're a lot more diluted than you thought you were.

ATER: Deluded?

REGGIE: Di-luted. More cream than coffee.

ATER: I don't understand.

REGGIE: The skin.

ATER: Oh, yes, I see. I notice black Americans are not very black.

REGGIE: Well, not compared to you.

ATER: Yes. Everyone stares at me on the street. In the airport.

REGGIE: Well, that's a part of the reason I came here, Ater. … I am saying it correctly.

ATER: Yes. Ater.

REGGIE: I know it's difficult, coming to such a foreign place. And I hate to say this, but not everyone you come across in the America will be as kind to you as the folks you've met the past few days. There are people here, ignorant people, who may laugh at the way you look, the way you talk.

ATER: Joseph and Deng have told me about this.

REGGIE: Yes. I wish— Well, I wish a lot of things, but you should know, if you come to Saint Bartholomew's you won't be an outsider. Everyone wants to do what they can to make you boys feel at home. I want you to feel welcome to stop by anytime.

ATER: Thank you.

REGGIE: And I know Mrs MacIntyre has been assigned to you, but I think it's always good to have a variety of resources. Maybe there are things you will feel more comfortable asking me.

ATER: Yes, okay.

REGGIE: And you can call me anytime. Day or night. The Lord has not blessed Lorraine and I with children of our own, so we—well, we've taken you all under our wing, /so to speak.

ATER: /I don't want to be rude, but I need to go back to the water closet.

REGGIE: Please. Don't let me stop you. I can let myself out.

ATER: *(Dashing off)* Yes, thank you. It is good to meet you. I'm sorry.

(Lights change, African music surges. The NAMELESS ONE *emerges, dancing, heading for* REGGIE *as he puts on his coat.* REGGIE *thinks he hears the music but he doesn't know where it's coming from. He can almost feel the* NAMELESS ONE. *She grabs his rosary from his pocket and dances around him twirling it. She takes a set of beads off her own neck and attaches the cross from his rosary to it. She slips it in his coat pocket as he heads to the door. Reaching for his gloves,* REGGIE *discovers the African beads. He is perplexed, slightly spooked. The* NAMELESS ONE *is very pleased.)*

Scene 4

*(*DIANE *sits in the comfy chair in the shrink's office. She is in mid-session.)*

DIANE: I keep thinking about my own obituary.

(Three beats on the drum)

DIANE: *(Angry)* I know it's morbid. But what would it say, really? "Diane MacIntyre: local benefactor, mother of one, widow of brilliant C E O."

(Light drumming)

DIANE: I don't know what I want it to say.

(Pause. A soft melancholy trumpet plays with the drum under the following.)

*(*DIANE, *half laughing at herself)*

DIANE: There was this moment, when we were in Africa—the first time—on safari…. I was convinced I was going to die. We were watching this pride of lions lazing under some trees. All of the sudden we could hear this distant trumpeting.

(The trumpet sings.)

DIANE: Our guide told us that groups of adolescent male elephants were banding together and wreaking havoc in the reserve: vandalizing property, ripping up trees and fences for no reason. Attacking tourists. They call them rogue elephants. Africa's newest malcontents.

Anyhow, we were standing there, in the truck.

(A low tremble of different drums)

DIANE: Waiting. I could feel the ground tremble.

(Again the trembling drums)

DIANE: Or I thought I could.

(Again)

DIANE: Maybe it was me.

(Again)

DIANE: Trembling.

(No music)

DIANE: I remember thinking, this would be an obituary I could live with.

Trampled to death by elephants in Africa.

(The drums crescendo with DIANE, but never obscure her words.)

DIANE: A quick and heroic sounding death. Not some furtive cancer that takes half your life before you even know it's gone. Not a bottle of Ativan washed down with vodka martinis. A death that people would talk about at benefits.

(Drumming ceases)

DIANE: "Did you hear about Diane? She was trampled by elephants. She died in Africa." *(Beat)* But no, Frank gets to die in Africa. He gets the half-page obituary and the exotic death.

Minus the elephants and the trampling.

(Four drum beats—a question)

DIANE: No, I'm not jealous. I don't know.

(Lights shift to ATER's apartment. ATER enters the space from the bathroom, followed by the NAMELESS ONE. He is wearing a winter jacket, though the sleeves are much too short on him. He lies down on the sofa. The NAMELESS ONE gently covers him with a blanket and tucks him in. Lights fade.)

Scene 5

(ATER is asleep on the sofa, tense, clutching one of the cushions. The NAMELESS ONE watches him, concerned. Loud white noise blares from the T V. It is day time. The door buzzer sounds, startling the NAMELESS ONE, but ATER does not stir. The buzzer sounds again after many seconds. No response. A minute later, a knock at the door.)

DIANE: *(Off stage)* Ater? Ater, are you home?

(ATER does not move. DIANE opens the front door, slowly. She spies ATER on the sofa.)

DIANE: There you are. Ater?

(DIANE enters and turns off the T V with the remote. She holds a bag of groceries in one hand.)

DIANE: Ater?

(DIANE shakes ATER's shoulder gently, but he starts, flailing, jumping up, scaring her.)

ATER: Ah! Ah! / Ah!

DIANE: /Oh! I'm sorry.

ATER: Diane.

DIANE: I didn't mean to startle you. Did you forget we were meeting?

(ATER *is disoriented. He looks at the T V. He still clutches the cushion.*)

ATER: No. I did not forget. I was sleeping.

DIANE: Yes, I noticed. Though I don't know how, with the T V on so loud.

ATER: Did you stop it?

DIANE: Yes.

(*Beat. The* NAMELESS ONE *inspects the groceries.*)

ATER: I thought maybe it ran out of sound.

DIANE: No. I turned it off.

ATER: I could not sleep. At night—the woman upstairs—her dog barks.

DIANE: All night?

ATER: No. Only sometimes. I will be sleeping and the dog will bark and I think, in my sleep, that I am back in my village. That we are being attacked by the Murahaleen, and our dogs have come to warn us, so we can run away and not be killed.

(*Beat.* NAMELESS ONE *looks at* ATER.)

DIANE: I can see how that might be disturbing.

ATER: I wake up and I have to remember where I am. It is difficult to sleep again, sometimes.

DIANE: What about your brothers, the rest of your group? Does the barking bother them, too?

ATER: (*Very matter of fact*) Joseph, yes. He sees the same things in his sleep when the dog barks. Deng, when Deng sleeps, nothing disturbs him. Abraham,… it was

not the same for him. He went to school many miles
from his village, a very long walk. One day he came
home and everyone was dead or run off.
*(He sets the cushion he's been holding, back in its proper
place on the sofa.)*

DIANE: Do you always sleep out here?

ATER: Yes. This is my spot. I have never slept alone
before, but there is no more room in the bedroom. With
the sound in the T V, I cannot hear the dog. I do not
have the dreams.

*(DIANE, unsettled by all this information, retreats to the
kitchen and unpacks her bag of groceries and cooking
paraphernalia.)*

DIANE: I thought I could show you how to make lentil
soup this morning, and then we could go to the bank
and set up an account for you.

ATER: I have a piece of paper from the government
they say is money.

DIANE: A check. Yes. I'll explain all about money today.
How is the job search going?

ATER: I have filled out many applications. No one has
hired me.

(DIANE spies a cutting board and sets it on the counter.)

DIANE: They will.
Here, I'll wash this celery and you can chop it up.

*(The NAMELESS ONE retreats. During the scene, DIANE
washes various vegetables and gives them to ATER to chop,
or goes through the cabinets.)*

DIANE: Okay, cut off the leafy parts and then cut it into
pieces about that big.

ATER: This soup will not make me sick?

DIANE: I don't think so. If we can find some foods that bridge the gap between what you ate in the camp, and regular, over-processed American food, maybe you won't have to be sick for a month like Abraham and Deng and Joseph were.

ATER: Yes, I would like to spend more time outside and not so much time in the bathroom. This is what they call it in America? The bathroom?

DIANE: Yes. *(Pause)* Ater? How old was Abraham? When his village was attacked?

ATER: Seven? Eight, maybe.

DIANE: He never found his family again?

ATER: He found refugees from another village as he walked. Sometimes we would meet an uncle or a cousin we had never seen before, when we came to a new village, but then the war would arrive and we would run again.

(DIANE takes a moment to digest this. She attempts to be casual, peeling a carrot.)

DIANE: What about your family? What happened to them? If you don't mind my asking.

ATER: *(Matter-of-factly, without emotion)* My father was killed by the Murahaleen, the Arab traitors. My younger brother was with me, but his feet got infected. I was too weak to carry him and he died. I do not know what happened to my mother or my sisters or my two older brothers. Maybe they are dead.

(Pause. DIANE is disturbed by this, but is not sure what to say. She pours some lentils into a measuring cup. ATER finishes chopping the celery.)

DIANE: At the camp, did they…did they have people who you could talk to about everything that happened to you? Psychologists or therapists?

ATER: There were counselors who asked us our stories. They wrote everything down.

DIANE: But did they help you?

ATER: I don't know what you mean.

DIANE: I mean, talking about what happened, to your brother, for instance, did that make you feel better?

ATER: No. This is done. What do you call it?

DIANE: Celery.

ATER: Celery.

DIANE: Now you can chop this carrot up into the same size pieces.

ATER: Okay.

DIANE: We have counselors here, too. Trained to help people who have experienced difficult things. You talk to them, tell them about what's happened to you. Because sometimes, even though you're not thinking about things, because you don't want to be sad, they seep in anyway, and come into your dreams or keep you up at night.

ATER: When you talk to the counselor, it doesn't make you feel worse?

DIANE: Well, sometimes it does, at first. But in the end it makes it better, I think. And then you don't have to sleep with the T V on.

ATER: Is that a bad thing? To sleep with the T V on?

DIANE: No, no. It's not bad. Lots of people do it. I do it myself.

ATER: For what reason do you do it?

DIANE: Well…I guess…. I suppose it's for the company. So I don't feel quite so alone.

ATER: You live by yourself?

DIANE: Yes. I do.

ATER: You do not have a husband?

(Beat)

DIANE: Not anymore.

ATER: *(Sensing her loss)* He is dead.

(Beat)

DIANE: Yes.

ATER: I can see in your face.
You were the first wife.

DIANE: Uhhh…no. I'm his second wife.

ATER: I thought, in America, men could only have a
first wife.

DIANE: No, well, they can have many wives, but
only one at a time. Frank was married when he was
younger, but he divorced. And then he married me.

ATER: So, the first wife is gone?

DIANE: Well, yes. She's not dead or anything, she lives
in Tahoe. This is the garlic. *(She crushes some garlic.)*

ATER: Does she make you call her mother?

DIANE: *(Amused)* No. No, I've never even met her.

ATER: May I ask how many children you have?

DIANE: Just Eve.

ATER: Only one child?

DIANE: Yes.

ATER: She is named after Eve in the Bible?

DIANE: No, well, it's spelled like that. You've read the
Bible?

ATER: Yes, of course. Your husband had no sons?

DIANE: No.

ATER: Will you have a son now? In his name?

DIANE: In his name? I don't understand what you mean. I'm too old to have children, now.

ATER: Then someone else should have a son in his name, so he can have an heir.

DIANE: He does have an heir. Eve is his heir.

ATER: Oh. My people, we believe that if you do not have a son, you cannot be an ancestor. If you don't have a son, you will die and be nothing.

DIANE: Well, that's not how it works here. Women have value in our culture.

ATER: Women have value in Dinka culture. A bride will bring a family many cows.

DIANE: Okay, so we're ready to start cooking. You put the heat on under the pot and add some oil, about that much, see? And then you put all the things you chopped up in there and you stir and cook until, until they're softer, but you want to be sure it doesn't burn. I typed it all up for you, so you don't have to remember, but it's good to know what it looks like as you go along.

ATER: Diane, you must tell me when I'm being rude. There are so many things I don't know. So many questions I have. I don't know when to stop asking.

DIANE: It's all right, Ater. No more questions about my family right now, okay?

ATER: Okay. May I ask about your hair?

DIANE: What about my hair?

ATER: Is it...? I see people here with blue hair. Pink hair. I know it is colored. Not real. But your hair. Does it come out of your head like that? Is it true?

DIANE: Well, yes, in a sense. This is exactly how it looked when I was younger. It's got a bit of silver in it now. My hairdresser covers it up and highlights it a little, but it's not quite the same as dying it blue. I like to think of it as restoring it to its former glory.

ATER: It looks like fire.

DIANE: Didn't any of the workers at the camp have red hair?

ATER: Yes, but I did not ever see them so close up.
(Beat)
May I touch it?

DIANE: …Yes. I guess so.

(ATER lays his hand on it gently.)

ATER: It is so soft.

(ATER runs his fingers through DIANE's hair, mesmerized. This unintentional intimacy brings sudden tears to DIANE's eyes. Though ATER doesn't notice her reaction he becomes uncomfortable after a moment and pulls his hand away.)

ATER: Thank you.

(DIANE surreptitiously wipes her eyes.)

DIANE: Of course.
Okay, where were we? Right, the lentils.

(Lights fade.)

Interlude

(Tinkly Musak plays. DIANE and ATER enter. They are shopping. DIANE hands ATER a stack of three polo shirts and holds open a door to a dressing room, ushers ATER inside, and closes the door behind him. ATER stands and regards himself in an imaginary mirror. He takes his shirt off. As he changes into a polo shirt the NAMELESS ONE enters the

stage. African drums begin to compete with the Musak.
ATER *looks in the mirror, pleased with how the new shirt*
looks. Then the NAMELESS ONE *steps into his mirror image*
and suddenly the shirt feels alien. The NAMELESS ONE
mirrors his movement as he runs his hand along the fabric.
ATER *reaches out to his image and she reaches back. Black*
out.)

Scene 6

(Lights up on EVE *and* ATER *in the car. She is driving. He*
is wearing the new shirt from the Interlude and is looking
sheepish.)

ATER: I am very sorry.

EVE: Ater, stop apologizing. It's not that big a deal.

ATER: Diane will be angry.

EVE: She'll be fine. She's the one who said we should
use her car.

ATER: I am sure she did not mean for me to crash it.

EVE: You didn't crash it. You…bumped it. It's a little
dent. She'll get it fixed and forget about it.

ATER: I will pay for it when I have the money.

EVE: She's not going to take your money.

(A silence as EVE *drives along.)*

ATER: Driving backwards is very different.

EVE: *(Smiling)* Yes.

ATER: It is a different thinking.

EVE: Yeah. *(Pulling over)* Is it all right if I drop you
here?

ATER: Yes.

Thank you again for giving me lessons. You are saving
me very much money.

EVE: It's no problem.

ATER: Abraham asks me if you will teach him too.

EVE: Oh. Well. Sure. I guess so.

ATER: Only if it is not... *(Searching for the word)*
...inconvenient.

EVE: No, it's good for me to have something
constructive to do. Get me out of the house.

ATER: I will tell him.
Okay. I will see you soon, I hope.

EVE: *(Blurting)* Can I ask you about your scars?

(ATER cracks a smile and brings a hand to his forehead.)

ATER: These scars?

EVE: Yeah.

ATER: It is the mark of my tribe. All the men from my
village have this mark.

EVE: So is it, like, identification?

ATER: Yes. It says where I am from, that I am a man
and a warrior.

(Beat)

EVE: How long have you had them?

ATER: I became a man when I was twelve. Some elders
at the camp, they made the blade and performed the
ceremony.

EVE: Did it hurt?

ATER: In a way, but I do not fully remember. In
our ceremony, you sit chanting the names of your
ancestors, over and over, so that you are in a sort of
dream. So that all you can hear is the names of your

fathers in your ears, until you cannot see, or taste, or feel. And when the knife cuts, it does not hurt. When the blood runs in your eyes you are not blinded. If you do not do it correctly, you will be aware and be afraid. If you are afraid, then you will pull away and the cut will not be complete. But they do not do it again. There is no second chance to be brave. And then your whole life you have the incomplete mark of a coward.

EVE: Wow. That's kinda hardcore.

ATER: Yes. The people at the camp, the relief workers, they do not want us to do this—I think because of infection—but some of us do it anyway, quietly, away from their eyes.

EVE: Well, it's totally cool-looking.

ATER: Americans are very curious about it.

EVE: Yeah, I'm sure. I hope you don't mind that I asked.

ATER: No.

EVE: People can be sensitive about their scars. You know, depending on how they got them.

ATER: Yes. Some of my scars, they are only for me to know the story of how they happened.

EVE: Yeah.
(Beat)
I have a scar like that.

(EVE *stares at* ATER *a moment, then pulls up her sleeve, revealing a thin white scar on her upper arm.*)

ATER: It's very old.

EVE: How do you know that?

ATER: Because it is stretched, like the ones on my legs.

EVE: Oh. Yeah. I guess so.
(She pulls her sleeve down.)

I'm not used to people looking at it.

ATER: Does it have shame? The scar?

EVE: No. It upsets my mother, so I don't…. I usually wear long sleeves. Even in the summer.

ATER: She knows the scar's story?

EVE: Part of it.
After all these years of seeing that fucking shrink, you'd think she'd be over it.

ATER: What is a shrink?

EVE: Oh, her therapist. Sorry.

ATER: Doctor Mazur.

EVE: *(Surprised)* Yeah.

ATER: Yes, she has made an appointment for me to talk to him.

EVE: Oh, Christ, you too? She's been trying to get *me* to go since I was—I mean, you should go, if you want to. It does help some people.

ATER: I am curious about it. We do not have anything like this in our culture.

EVE: I bet she offered to pay, huh?

ATER: Yes.

EVE: Typical.

ATER: May I look at your scar again?

(Beat)

EVE: Sure.

(EVE *pulls up her sleeve and* ATER *carefully runs his finger down her scar.*)

ATER: It is funny how, on white people, the scars are lighter than the skin and on black skin scars are darker.

(EVE *glances at* ATER*'s forehead.*)

EVE: Yeah, that's weird, huh?

(Lights fade.)

Interlude

(The transition, the sounds of el train on the tracks, horns honking, elephants trumpeting, hooves stampeding, drumming. ATER and the NAMELESS ONE traverse the stage in a rhythmic walking dance. At the end: a tiny ding of an egg timer.)

Scene 7

(Lights up on ATER's apartment. DIANE pulls a tray of oatmeal cookies out of the oven and puts a new tray in. She is fidgety, nervous. She looks at her watch, chews her lip.)

(There is a knock at the door.)

DIANE: Ater?

(REGGIE opens the door. He holds a book wrapped in cloth. DIANE's discomfort level increases. She's a bit manic.)

REGGIE: Hello?

DIANE: Oh. Deacon Hudson. Hello.

REGGIE: Mrs MacIntyre.

DIANE: I thought you might be Ater.

REGGIE: He's not here?

DIANE: No. We had an appointment today, to meet. He's been late before, but never this late. I'm a bit concerned to tell you the truth.

REGGIE: Are the other boys home?

DIANE: No. I think they're at work.

REGGIE: You have a key?

DIANE: No. No. He, none of them, ever lock the door. I keep telling them it's not safe, they don't seem to— Even the door downstairs is always propped open. I want to close it, but Joseph told me he's been locked out twelve times.

REGGIE: Yes. I noticed the door. That's how I got in.

DIANE: Yes. *(She looks at her watch.)*

REGGIE: How long have you been waiting?

DIANE: Almost two hours.

REGGIE: That is late.

DIANE: Did you have an appointment with him as well? He didn't tell me, but he wouldn't necessarily.

REGGIE: Yes. No. I don't have an appointment. I was just checking in, dropping off a new Bible for him.

DIANE: I see.

(The oven timer dings.)

DIANE: Oh, that's the cookies, they're probably not done yet, this batch, I don't trust the oven so I've been setting the timer conservatively, no, they're not done, *(Beat)* but these have been cooling for a while. If you'd like one.

REGGIE: You're making cookies?

DIANE: Well, that was part of our plan for the day. But I got nervous. Waiting. If I don't occupy myself with something, I start thinking of scenarios.

REGGIE: Scenarios?

DIANE: You know, maybe he got hit by a bus, or stabbed by thugs, or attacked by dogs. Or maybe he's just lost, but that one doesn't stick with me for more than a moment or two, because, you know, it's far too logical and not nearly morbid enough.

REGGIE: I see.

DIANE: It's a mother thing. *(Beat)* Please have a cookie. They're oatmeal raisin. No nuts, if you're allergic.

REGGIE: Thank you. Still warm.

DIANE: Yes.

(Awkward pause as REGGIE *chews.)*

REGGIE: Very good.

DIANE: *(Cautiously, but condescending)* You should have had some tea.

REGGIE: Pardon me?

DIANE: Last time you were here, Ater gave you some tea, but you didn't drink any. He told me.

REGGIE: I don't particularly like tea.

DIANE: I tried to explain that you didn't mean any offense. It's considered rude in Dinka culture to refuse an offering of food.

REGGIE: I didn't realize that.

DIANE: I told him that sometimes people say "no thank you," and it's perfectly acceptable. I think the concept of refusing food is a little hard to get your mind around if you're from a country where no one has enough to eat. Anyhow, it's not so much to ask that we meet him halfway on some of these things, especially at first. We don't want to be arrogant, and pretend that our way is the only way, after all.

REGGIE: *(As polite as he can manage)* No, of course. Thank you for telling me.

(Awkward pause)

DIANE: You could leave the Bible for him. If you don't want to wait.

REGGIE: Well, I have to admit, I'm a little concerned myself, now.

DIANE: The other volunteers, they did tell me about the tardiness issue, but still, this seems extreme.

REGGIE: Yes.

DIANE: Do you think we should call the police?

REGGIE: Why don't we give it another half hour.

(The oven timer dings again. DIANE *checks the cookies and takes the second tray out.)*

REGGIE: I wonder, Mrs MacIntyre, if baking cookies is the best use of your time.

DIANE: What does that mean?

REGGIE: It's just not a usual volunteer-refugee activity. Helping him set up a bank account, showing him the library—

DIANE: We've done those things. I thought teaching him how to make inexpensive, healthy food was useful.

REGGIE: No, it is. *(Beat)* How often do you see Ater?

DIANE: About once a week.

REGGIE: I heard you bought him some clothes.

DIANE: The donated clothes don't fit him.

REGGIE: It's not really appropriate—

DIANE: To let him walk around in pants that are two inches too short? You're right. It's not appropriate. He didn't even have a decent pair of gloves. This is Chicago, these boys think fifty degrees is cold. I bought them all gloves, if you want to know.

(Beat)

REGGIE: That was very generous of you.

DIANE: It's not a matter of generosity, it's a matter of practicality.

REGGIE: Perhaps, next time, it would be better to donate the clothes to the church and we can distribute them.

DIANE: I see.

REGGIE: We just wouldn't want you to get into a position where the boys started asking you for things. Putting you on the spot.

DIANE: Oh.
So, you're protecting me?

REGGIE: Yes.

(DIANE *nods. A pause.* REGGIE *sits on the sofa and unwraps the Bible.*)

DIANE: *(Quietly)* What is that you have it wrapped in?

REGGIE: An African cloth.

DIANE: Is it Kenyan?

REGGIE: ...I'm not sure. My wife gave it to me.

DIANE: It looks similar to the cloth they wrap their dead in.

REGGIE: Are you a scholar of textiles? or of African culture.

DIANE: Neither. Just a little detail I picked up there on my last trip.

REGGIE: I see. My wife and I would love to go someday. We couldn't afford it as a vacation, but perhaps as missionaries.

DIANE: It's really not that expensive, once you get there. It's the tickets.

REGGIE: Yes. I'm sure.

(Awkward pause)

DIANE: How long have you worked for the church?

REGGIE: Ten years.

DIANE: Have you done much missionary work?

REGGIE: Not abroad, though I'd like to.

DIANE: Why?

REGGIE: Why? You mean aside from spreading the word of the Lord?

DIANE: Yes.

REGGIE: Well…to travel. See a bit of the world. Learn about other cultures.

DIANE: You know, I don't know that much about missionary work, but from my understanding of it, there's not much focus on learning about other cultures.

REGGIE: What is the focus? As you see it?

DIANE: I don't think we should talk about this. Like I said, I don't know much about what missionaries do.

REGGIE: But that's why I'm asking. It's good to know what the misconceptions are.

DIANE: If you already view my opinion as a "misconception" then there's not much point in my saying anything.

REGGIE: That was the wrong choice of words. I would like to hear the perspective, the perceptions of a non-religious person. Would that be the proper classification?

DIANE: Yes.

REGGIE: If you feel comfortable sharing your thoughts with me.

(Beat)

DIANE: All right.

I think Christian missionaries corrupt and homogenize other cultures with the white man's religion. Don't you think it's bad enough that your ancestors were torn from their homes, divided, oppressed, denied the right to practice their own indigenous religions and force-fed Christianity in its stead? Is it really necessary that you continue the brainwashing?

(*Beat*)

REGGIE: Well. I can't say I see it as brainwashing.

DIANE: I'm sorry, Deacon Hudson, but I think it's appalling that you pounce on these refugees the moment they get off the plane, flinging Bibles at them, hardly giving them the chance to recover from the missionaries at Kakuma.

REGGIE: Recover?

DIANE: Why can't you let them be who they are? It's bad enough that your ancestors had their culture stripped away, but to do the same thing to your own people, three hundred years after the fact— It shows no respect for the Dinka way of life.

(REGGIE *takes a deep breath, trying to be patient.*)

REGGIE: Ms MacIntyre—

DIANE: Mrs.

REGGIE: Mrs.
Christianity *is* part of the Dinka culture. Ater's entire village practiced Catholicism. Some of the refugees are Episcopalian, Lutheran…each village had a church.

DIANE: Started by Western missionaries.

REGGIE: Yes. Started long before any of these boys were born. Ater was baptized as a baby, confirmed at the refugee camp. Catholicism is part of who he is.

DIANE: Don't you think that's sad?

REGGIE: *(Somewhat amused)* No. I don't. Why would I?

DIANE: Well, I do. I think it's very sad that Western culture is so insidious that it reaches into the very depths of a country and tells perfectly innocent people that they're going to hell if they don't believe in Jesus.

REGGIE: That's a rather simplistic view of our mission, don't you think? We provide health care, education—

DIANE: At what cost? Do you know how much has been lost due to the oppression by Christian missionaries? The history, the indigenous religions, the languages.

REGGIE: Have we ruined Ater for you? Is he not authentic enough?

DIANE: Excuse me?

REGGIE: I think, perhaps, Mrs MacIntyre, that you are merely disappointed that Ater isn't the noble savage you thought he would be.

DIANE: That's ridiculous.

REGGIE: Is it? Are you going to tell me that you didn't have some overly romanticized idea in your head of an innocent chased out of some non-existent tribal utopia and dropped into your world for your amusement?

DIANE: That is really offensive.

REGGIE: Well, I think you telling me about my ancestors is offensive.

DIANE: I was defending them.

REGGIE: Well, it's Not. Your. Place. Nor is it your place to be outraged by Ater's religion or my attempts to make him feel welcome at the parish. Catholicism, Jesus, is one of the few constants in his life. Would you have us deny him a sense of community, something these boys so desperately need? Would you have me cast them away, close our doors to them, because I now represent the legacy of colonial imperialism? Don't you dare think the irony is lost on me, Mrs MacIntyre. I understand the source of your outrage, but, in this instance, I assure you, it is wholly misplaced.

(Before DIANE *can respond,* ATER *enters with the* NAMELESS ONE, *happy—a bounce in his step.)*

ATER: Hello! Ah, Deacon Hudson. I did not know you were coming.

DIANE: Ater! Where have you been?

ATER: I am late, then?

DIANE: Almost two hours.

ATER: What is that smell?

REGGIE: Ater, where have you been?

ATER: I was walking. I met some people. These smell wonderful. What are they?

(While ATER *inspects the cookies, the* NAMELESS ONE *inspects the Bible.)*

DIANE: Oatmeal cookies. I was going to show you how to make them—

ATER: What are the black things?

DIANE: Raisins.

ATER: What are raisins?

DIANE: They're dried grapes. Dried fruit.

*(*ATER *tastes the cookie.)*

ATER: This is very good.

REGGIE: Ater, I just stopped by to drop off a new Bible for you.

ATER: Oh, thank you.

REGGIE: But I should go now.

ATER: No, wait, I must tell you both about the warriors I met.

(DIANE *and* REGGIE *exchange a confused look.*)

ATER: Each day after I apply for three jobs, I walk to see a different neighborhood. Today I went to Garfield Park.

REGGIE: You didn't walk all the way from Garfield Park.

ATER: Yes, there and back.

DIANE: That's miles away.

ATER: It is not so far.

DIANE: But Ater, that's not a very safe neighborhood.

ATER: This is what I find out. I am walking and I notice there are these men, they are following me. Everyone is looking at me, but this is usual, for people here to look at me. I decide to stop walking. I think I can run faster than these men, but I am not sure, and I want to know why they stalk me like I am a gazelle. So, one of them—I think he is the leader—comes up to me and asks me who I am, why I am in their neighborhood. They do not believe me at first, that I am from Africa. They have never heard of the Republic of Sudan. But when they understand, they are very nice, show me their sign. Is there a war of some kind?

REGGIE: Those boys are members of a gang, Ater.

DIANE: *(To* ATER*)* They're criminals, at war with other criminals.

(DIANE *and* REGGIE *are barely maintaining civility.*)

REGGIE: Perhaps you're not the best person to educate Ater about gang violence., Mrs MacIntyre.

DIANE: You're right, I'm not. Will you stay and do it, please?

REGGIE: Maybe another time. I wouldn't want to disrupt your plans.

DIANE: My plans have already been disrupted. I'm sorry, Ater, but I have an appointment in an hour, and anyway, I baked the cookies. Without you. While I was waiting.

ATER: I'm sorry, Diane.

DIANE: Look, it's all right. We'll just have to plan to meet on days when my schedule is more open. And maybe you'll have to start wearing that watch we bought and looking at it. Meanwhile, the Deacon can stay and talk with you for a bit and give you your new Bible. I'll call you tomorrow.

ATER: Okay. Thank you for the cookies.

DIANE: Maybe you should highlight the undesirable areas on a map for him.

REGGIE: I'm not sure that my definition of undesirable is the same as yours.

DIANE: I'm sure it's not. And I'm sure you think that makes me a terrible person, too. (*She leaves, slamming the door.*)

ATER: You have been arguing.

REGGIE: I don't want you to worry about that. We just had a little disagreement.

ATER: About me?

REGGIE: No.

ATER: You look very angry.

REGGIE: I'm fine.

ATER: Your face is all red—I did not know brown skin would do this.

REGGIE: Ater.

ATER: You don't like Diane.

REGGIE: I don't know her.

ATER: But you do not like her anyway.

REGGIE: She doesn't like me, Ater.

ATER: She is afraid of you, I think.

REGGIE: What? No, she's not.

ATER: She's very nervous around you. She is not like this with me. Why are you so angry with her, when you have so much more?

REGGIE: More? More what?

ATER: You are a man of God. You have a place of respect in the community.

REGGIE: Yeah. Well, Ater, we Men of God don't have the same status in America as we do some other places. In our own religious community, of course, we're respected, but not necessarily in the community at large. Unfortunately, in America, money is what most people respect.

ATER: Does Diane have more money than you?

REGGIE: Yes, I'm sure she does.

ATER: How do you know her wealth?

REGGIE: (Searching a bit) …Because of the clothes she wears, the way she talks, the fact that she's got time to help you and doesn't have a job.

ATER: So, she is more important than you?

(Beat)

REGGIE: In some people's eyes.

ATER: And that is why you don't like her.

REGGIE: Look, Ater, enough about Mrs MacIntyre. I want you to tell me about these men you met this afternoon. What did you mean when you said they showed you're their sign.

ATER: They say this is how they know you are a friend. *(He awkwardly flashes him a gang sign.)*

REGGIE: Okay, first of all, don't ever do that again.

ATER: It is bad?

REGGIE: Yes, in a way. More importantly, it doesn't have anything to do with you and you shouldn't be doing it. It's a gang sign. And when you do it, you're saying that you're a member of the gang.

ATER: Like my scars say that I am a member of my tribe.

REGGIE: …sort of.

ATER: So a gang is like a tribe.

REGGIE: No, Ater, it's not the same. And if you make that gang sign in front of the wrong people….

ATER: Someone will shoot me?

REGGIE: Possibly.

ATER: The elders, at Kakuma, they tell us about these gangs, tell us to stay away from them.

REGGIE: Then why didn't you?

ATER: Because at Kakuma we hear many, many things about America—that a black man would get shot for even holding the hand of a white woman, but I see this all the time in Chicago. Many things we heard about, I can see they are not true. So when I meet these boys, I think, maybe they are a gang, but I decide to learn what this means with my own eyes. They are warriors. Like me.

REGGIE: No, Ater, they are not like you. These gangs they divide us and bring us down, instead of uniting us. They spread fear and death to their own people.

ATER: Like the Dinka and the Nuer.

REGGIE: No. Well…maybe.

ATER: Two groups, looking the same, having similar culture, but fighting each other over land and weakening themselves while the government grows fat and strong, ready to destroy us.

REGGIE: Yes, there are parallels.

ATER: Will you explain to me more about these gangs?

REGGIE: Of course.

ATER: Would you like some tea? We can have it with the cookies.

REGGIE: Yes, let's discuss gang violence over tea and cookies. I think that's a grand idea.

(Lights fade.)

Scene 8

(Lights up on the chair in the shrink's office. ATER sits in it, looking uncomfortable. The NAMELESS ONE stands nearby. Before her stands a trunk standing on its end. Upon it is a bowl of water.)

ATER: So, I am supposed to talk to you?

(Five drum beats)

ATER: About what?

(Drumming)

ATER: There are things, things that are difficult here. But I have food and a place to live. No one is trying to kill me in America.

(More drumming)

ATER: When I left my home? You mean when my village was attacked?

(One drum beat. Throughout the following the NAMELESS
ONE *slowly and very methodically draws tears on her face
with the water.)*

ATER: *(Unemotional)* Yes, I remember it. When the dogs
woke us, I knew right away what was happening: the
Murahaleen had finally come.

There was gunfire and screaming. I was outside,
running, before I was truly awake, I think. When I got
to a place where I could hide in the elephant grass—I
stopped. To see.

Only my little brother Lual was with me. I was looking
for my family, to see which way they had gone. People
were being shot, falling. Homes burning.

My father was yelling, telling us to run. He was hurt,
calling from the ground.

There was this moment. It seemed very long, though
it could not have been. I knew if we stayed we would
die, but to run away from everyone and everything we
had known....

(As if it did not happen to him)

How do you do this? Is it not its own kind of dying?
Once you are running, it is not so difficult. It is making
the decision to take that first step, a step you cannot
ever take back. That is the hardest part.

(The lights partially fade on ATER *and shift. A doorbell
rings. The* NAMELESS ONE *places the bowl on the ground
and removes the cloth from the "table" revealing a small
trunk. She lays it down on the floor as* DIANE *enters. She is
momentarily frozen by the sight of the trunk. Then she opens
it revealing a box of ashes, wrapped in a cloth similar to the
one* REGGIE *carried.* DIANE *stares at the ashes, transfixed.
She lowers herself to her knees. The* NAMELESS ONE *tries to
lead* DIANE'S *hands to the box,* DIANE *cannot bring herself
to touch it. Practically begging* DIANE *to express something,
the* NAMELESS ONE *paints tears on* DIANE'S *face with*

the water. DIANE *does not react, does not even feel it, and nothing appears on her face. Drums swell. Black out.)*

END OF ACT ONE

ACT TWO

Entr'acte

(*Lights up on the foyer of the* MACINTYRE *house. African masks hang high on the walls and a Dinka spear and shield are displayed in a small alcove. A box filled with belongings—both* EVE's *and her father's—sits near the door. The* NAMELESS ONE *enters dancing. When she sees the box she stops, peeks inside. She pulls out a man's wristwatch, looks at it curiously and drops it back in. She pulls out a man's flannel shirt, smells it, drops back in. Then she lifts out a tulle skirt with a ribbon. She inspects it. Classical music seeps in competing with the African music. She ties the skirt around her waist. She tries a few ballet steps, a pirouette. She peers back into the box and pulls out a teddy bear. She twirls around a bit, the bear her dance partner then waves off the classical music and resumes her African dance. She spies a set of cars keys and jangles them in beat to the music. Voices can be heard approaching. Taking the keys, she leaps through the window and freezes on the pedestal. Lights change into:*)

Scene 9

DIANE: (*Off stage*) Look, I don't want to get into a big thing about it—

(EVE *enters carrying a box of books.* DIANE *follows holding the box of ashes.*)

DIANE: —I just want to leave the ashes here. They don't feel right in my apartment.

EVE: Of course they don't feel right. You're not supposed to keep them in your home, constantly reminding you every moment of the day. You're supposed to lay them to rest.

DIANE: I'm not prepared to make a decision about that right now.

EVE: You don't need to be prepared, you need to follow his wishes. He wanted to be buried.

DIANE: In the back yard, which is clearly not happening now.

EVE: I think it's a sign that you shouldn't sell the house.

DIANE: It's not a "sign," Eve, and your father is not going to dictate where I live from the grave.

EVE: I can't believe how easily you're dismissing what he wanted. Dad wanted to be buried next to the elm tree so he could become part of life again.

DIANE: Maybe we could scatter him in Lake Michigan.

EVE: *(With doorbell ringing)* No!

DIANE: Good lord, he's early.

EVE: Give him to me.
(She takes the ashes and stomps off into the house.)

DIANE: You should say hello to Ater. He'll want to see you.

(DIANE opens the front door. ATER stands outside wearing a rather loud basketball jersey and matching sweat pants, as well as a baseball cap worn at a jaunty angle.)

ATER: Hello, Diane. I am on time.

DIANE: Yes, you are. Where on earth did you get those clothes?

ATER: Here. In Chicago. With my first paycheck. They are American clothes.

DIANE: Your…your other clothes are American, too.

ATER: Yes, but…these are the first clothes I have ever bought for myself. People do not stare at me so much when I wear them.

DIANE: That's hard to believe.
Come in. I'm almost ready to go. You didn't have any trouble finding the house?

ATER: No, it was—
(He sees the masks for the first time.)
Where did you get these?

DIANE: Oh…well, two of them I bought on our first trip to Africa, and the rest I got from dealers in the states.

ATER: Why do you have them on your wall?

DIANE: Well…to display them. They're works of art.

ATER: They are ceremonial masks. And this is someone's spear and shield. To be carried.

(Beat)

DIANE: Is it insulting? To have them on the wall?

ATER: Insulting is not the right word. Why do they have importance for you?

DIANE: Well, I…because they remind me of what a beautiful place it is, what a wonderful time we had there. I fell in love with Africa, the first time we went. Everything about it: the taste of the air and the angle of the sunlight…. It created this…euphoria inside me. Maybe it's one of those things that happens to you on vacation, but I wanted to bring Africa back home with me, so I wouldn't forget how it made me feel, so I bought these masks.
Does that make any sense?

ATER: Only the part about the taste of the air. What is vacation?

DIANE: Why don't I explain it on the way to the museum. I just need to run upstairs for a moment.

(DIANE *exits.* ATER *inspects the shield and spear, then looks out the window.*)

ATER: There is a girl outside.

(*The* NAMELESS ONE, *posed as the Statue, turns and looks at him, though he is not looking at her.*)

DIANE: (*Off stage*) Oh, the Statue. Doesn't she look real? She used to fool me, for years.

ATER: No, there is a real girl. She is digging in the ground. I think maybe it is Eve.

DIANE: (*Off stage*) What? Eve! What are you doing? You're not burying /the ashes—

EVE: (*Off stage*) /No, Jesus, Mom. I'm digging up some plants.

(DIANE *tries to maintain a veneer of civility.*)

DIANE: (*Off stage*) Eve— ! Will you come inside, please? Say hello to Ater.

(ATER *picks up the teddy bear and inspects it.* EVE *enters. Her hands and clothing are slightly smudged with dirt. She has taken off her outer shirt revealing a small tattoo of a green snake on her upper arm. She is amused by his clothes.*)

EVE: Oh. Ater, hi.

ATER: Hello, Eve.

EVE: Nice threads.

ATER: Threads? Oh. Thank you. I don't think your mother likes them.

EVE: It doesn't matter if she likes them. It only matters if you like them.

I hear she's taking you to the museum.

ATER: Yes. Diane is letting me drive. So I can practice.

EVE: It sounds like quite an adventure.

ATER: Are you coming with us?

EVE: No. No…I've been on the Diane MacIntyre
museum tour many times.

ATER: She says she wants me to see African Art and
Western Art in the same context. I don't know what
this means.

EVE: Trust me, she'll talk your ear off for three hours
and you still won't know what it means.

ATER: It is strange to me, this American idea of art. We
do not have this in my culture, pretty things used only
for decoration and scenery. There is purpose behind
everything. But in America you take something that
you will never use, that you do not know how to use,
something that is not part of your own history, and
you hang it on the wall.

EVE: Yeah, well, I'm sure she'll sell you the party line
about preservation, but the truth is: Westerners like to
steal things.

ATER: *(Indicating the teddy bear)* Is this artwork also?

EVE: Him? No. That's Brutus. I'm…boxing up some of
my stuff since Mom is selling the house.

ATER: Brutus?

EVE: He's a teddy bear.
You don't know what that is, do you.

ATER: It is a toy?

EVE: Well, yeah, he's a toy, but he's a friend, too. I took
him to bed with me every night for years. Couldn't
sleep without him.

ATER: Does he chase away evil spirits?

EVE: I don't know about that. He was comforting, made me feel less alone. When you're an only child, sometimes all you have are inanimate objects to sympathize with you when your parents are losing their minds.

ATER: He helps you sleep? I have trouble sleeping.

EVE: Oh. Well. Yeah, I mean... *(Snatching Brutus away, clutching him)* You have to know him, he's not magic or anything. He's just crusted up with years of snot-nosed weeping.
(Beat)
I'm sorry. I don't mean to be—

ATER: I was not suggesting that I take him. I was only curious.

EVE: No. I know. He was a gift from my father, that's all.

(The NAMELESS ONE *has left the pedestal and crept closer.)*

ATER: *(Indicating the box)* All of these things...they are from your father also?

EVE: No, not all, some... This was his watch, not his nice watch, his gardening watch, all scratched. And this shirt, it still smells like him.... It's stupid.

ATER: You miss your father.

EVE: Yes.

ATER: Yes. I miss my father too.

(Three beats. DIANE *enters. The* NAMELESS ONE *feels the moment of connection break.)*

DIANE: What are you doing to the yard, dear?

EVE: I'm taking some of the things Dad and I planted together.

DIANE: You're not going to leave it like—

EVE: No, Mom. I'm not. I'll make sure it looks up to the neighborhood standards.

DIANE: Good because the realtor is coming to see the place this weekend— *(Seeing her arm)* Oh you didn't.

(EVE, realizing, reflexively covers the tattoo.)

EVE: Mom, I don't/ want to—

DIANE: /Tell me you didn't.

EVE: Can we not get into this right now?

DIANE: *(Overlapping)* The piercings were one thing, but a tattoo?

EVE: It's just a little green tree snake, see? It's nothing horrific.

(ATER looks increasingly uncomfortable. The NAMELESS ONE covers her ears, pained.)

DIANE: It's never coming off.

EVE: Yes, mother. I'm aware.

DIANE: Were you sober when you did this?

EVE: Yes, Jesus, Mom. I was sober. They did a nice job, don't you think?

DIANE: Couldn't you have at least done it on the other arm, covered the—

EVE: Do NOT make this about / my scar.

ATER: /Do not argue. Please.

(They all turn and look at ATER. A pause)

EVE: I'm sorry, Ater.

DIANE: We should get down to the museum.

(No one moves. Lights change.)

Interlude

(EVE *exits quietly. The* NAMELESS ONE *jumps in and hits the unlock button on the car keys.* ATER *and* DIANE *begin to move to the car. The* NAMELESS ONE *tries to hand the keys to* DIANE *who ignores her. The* NAMELESS ONE *gives the keys to* ATER. DIANE *and* ATER *situate themselves in the car as the* NAMELESS ONE *gets in the back seat.*)

Scene 10

(*Lights up on* DIANE *and* ATER *in the car.* ATER *is driving cautiously.* DIANE *is clearly still upset. There is a stony silence. The* NAMELESS ONE *rides in the back seat.*)

DIANE: Watch out for that— !
You have to be very careful around cyclists, Ater. They're unpredictable.

ATER: Thank you.

DIANE: You'll want to make a left at the light. That's the most direct route.

ATER: Okay.

(*Pause*)

DIANE: So, how is your job?

ATER: It is okay. Very warm. I take the towels and sheets out of the dryers and fold them.

DIANE: It sounds like that could get rather boring.

ATER: It is not exciting, but I have started classes at the university. I have many things to think about, while I fold my towels.

DIANE: Are the people at the hotel, your co-workers, are they nice to you?

ATER: Yes, they are nice. They have some very strange ideas about Africa. They do not seem to understand that it is a very big place with many kinds of people. They do not know about the war.

DIANE: No. I think you'll find most Americans are completely ignorant about almost everything.

ATER: I want to ask you: Is it bad, wrong, to work quickly?

DIANE: No. Well, maybe if working quickly makes you sloppy or dangerous.

ATER: One of the other workers, DeShawn, he says I make him look bad, that I am too serious, working too hard. But I do not think he works hard enough. He is always talking to the girls, making jokes, only doing his job Mister Childers comes through. I think this is wrong, because they pay us to work, not to talk only, and there is nothing to stop us from talking while we work. There is no rule against this. *(Beat)* What is a patsy?

DIANE: A patsy?

ATER: He says I am a patsy. DeShawn. That we are only cleaning white towels for rich white people to make dirty again, that they are not worth working hard for, that the black man has already worked hard enough for the white man. This does not make any sense, because Renee and Mike, they are white and they fold towels, though I do not think they work very hard either.

I do not like folding towels. It is not exciting. But it is my job and I do it and they pay me. I know I will not always be there. And it is much better than doing nothing. I had many years of nothing at Kakuma. Many days when I would have been glad to fold someone's towels. But I say nothing to DeShawn because I think he will not understand me.

DIANE: You know what, Ater? DeShawn has his reasons for being angry. I don't know that he's right, but he has his reasons. But I don't think you should let his feelings, his history, effect how you do your job. Okay?

ATER: Yes, thank you.

DIANE: Sure.
CAREFUL THAT'S A STOP SIGN!

(*A screech of tires.* DIANE *grips her seat.*)

ATER: I'm sorry. Are you hurt?

DIANE: I'm fine.

(*A car honks from behind.* ATER *drives on. Pause*)

ATER: Eve says you don't drive.

DIANE: Well, I can, but no, I don't really. Not in the city.

ATER: Why?

DIANE: I guess I've never gotten accustomed to it.

ATER: Can I ask why you are angry about Eve's tattoo?

DIANE: I think it's better if we don't talk about it.

ATER: Is it because her name is Eve that she got the snake?

DIANE: No, I…
I have no idea why she got it.

ATER: In Dinka culture we have a goddess called Abuk. She is like Eve in the Bible, she is the first woman. Her symbol is a snake.

DIANE: Ater, I'd really rather not talk /discuss it.

ATER: /I am sorry, Diane. I don't understand why it hurts you. This tattoo.

DIANE: I don't know either.

ATER: Maybe because you were not there to see her get it?

DIANE: You should pay attention to the road. It gets a little windy up here.

ATER: Okay.

(A silence. DIANE turns on the radio. Classical music plays, something by Haydn.)

ATER: What do you do in America, when a child becomes an adult? What sort of ceremony do you have?

DIANE: Well…Jews have bar mitzvahs or bat mitzvahs, if they're religious. Catholics have confirmation. I don't know what else.

ATER: At what age?

DIANE: Around thirteen.

ATER: Is it a public ceremony?

DIANE: Usually. But it's symbolic. The ceremony. No one really considers them adults. They're still children.

ATER: Why do you have a ceremony bringing a person into adulthood, and then not allow them to be adults. What is the point?

DIANE: It's not that they're not allowed. They're not ready. They're very old ceremonies, Ater. People got married, had children, at a much earlier age back then. It's merely a tradition now. Slow down he's turning!

ATER: So at what age do Americans become adults now?

DIANE: …It depends. Whenever they live separately from their parents, support themselves financially. For some it's as early as seventeen or eighteen. For some… never, almost.

ATER: How do you know when someone has had a ceremony?

DIANE: You ask them, I guess.

ATER: There is no way to tell by looking at them? No mark or tattoo?

DIANE: No. What are you getting at, Ater?

ATER: Getting at?

DIANE: What are you trying to say?

ATER: You have never asked me about the scars on my forehead.

DIANE: *(Beat)* I read about it.

ATER: Do you find it distasteful?

DIANE: To be honest, a bit, yes.

ATER: I am surprised you feel this way, Diane. I am preserving my culture.

DIANE: Yes. You are,/ but —

ATER: /But I should only preserve the culture that is not distasteful?

DIANE: No, Ater. It's just difficult for me. I can't help seeing it as mutilation. You're driving a little too far to the right, you need to /center yourself—

ATER: /It is not mutilation. It is my identification and my identity and it cannot be erased. Perhaps this is what the snake is to Eve.

DIANE: Ater, it's different here. We don't have those sorts of rituals.

ATER: I do not think this is true. Those men that I met on the street that day. They showed me they all had the same tattoo.

DIANE: What men? The gang kids?

ATER: Yes. It is their way of saying who they are.

DIANE: It's their way of indelibly marking themselves with hatred. Not so fast, okay?

ATER: And a girl at the hotel laundry, she has these dark lines on her arms. Very straight. I ask her what they are from. She says she cuts herself, with a razor blade—

DIANE: Ater...

ATER: —watches the blood come to the surface so she can see what is inside of her.

DIANE: That's not ritual, Ater. That's a sickness. She does that because she's in pain. And she ought to get some help.

ATER: I think there must be a need to mark ourselves.

DIANE: You really ought to use your turn signals when you change lanes.

ATER: I am trying to learn what the rituals are in America. They are very well hidden and different for everyone, it seems.

DIANE: Yes...

ATER: Why doesn't you husband have a grave?

DIANE: What?

ATER: Eve said—

DIANE: I only got his ashes back a few weeks ago, Ater. I don't—I haven't— haven't had time....

ATER: But you will bury him.

DIANE: Ater.

ATER: This is what Americans do. I'm asking.

DIANE: It's what some people do. Most people.

ATER: What do your people do?

DIANE: My people.

(Pause)

I don't know who "my people" are, Ater.

(Pause)

ATER: We bury our dead. My people. When we can.

(DIANE *nods. Pause)*

ATER: So many…died during our walking.
We could not stop. We could not say goodbye. There
was no time for ritual, no strength…
We could not spare any energy for prayer or sadness.
Only for moving our feet. If you gave over to sadness
you would stop moving, and then you too would die.
I think this is what Doctor Mazur meant when he said
I do not have the luxury to "be in touch with my pain."
It's a funny expression.

DIANE: You saw Ben?

ATER: Yes. Once.

DIANE: Strange, he didn't charge— Did he help you?

ATER: He is very nice. I told him my whole life story.
He says that I have had more, he calls them "traumatic
experiences," than anyone he has ever met.

DIANE: But did it make you feel better? To talk about
it?

ATER: No. He says I am…"emotionally disassociated."
Usually, it is bad to be disassociated, but he says in my
case it's good. He says that if I was not disassociated
I would not get out of bed in the morning. I cannot
imagine this, but I believe him, because I have seen it,
with some of the others. He says, right now, I cannot
afford to come back to talk to him about my history.

DIANE: I'll pay. I'd be happy/ to pay.

ATER: /He is afraid I will stop functioning, Diane,
like the ones who sat down and died on the way to
Ethiopia. My feet must keep moving...still.
He says I should live my new life. I have lived one
whole life in Africa, and now my new life is here in
America, and it should not be so hard.
I think I will be able to associate with my life here.

(The lights change.)

Interlude

*(As DIANE exits, the NAMELESS ONE sits next to ATER. She
hands him a letter that ATER regards with unease. After a
moment he reads it. He is disturbed by its contents. He rises,
folds the letter back up. The NAMELESS ONE watches ATER
place it under his pillow on the sofa. The lights fade.)*

Scene 11

*(Lights up on the shrink's office. This time EVE sits in the
chair looking a bit uncomfortable.)*

EVE: Okay, you know...maybe this was a really bad
idea. I mean, you shouldn't go to your mother's shrink,
right? Because already you're not objective. Already
everything you hear come out of my mouth is colored
by what my mother's said about me. I mean, that
wasn't a criticism. I'm not judging your professional
abilities. I'm just saying...it's inevitable. I don't plan
on making a habit out of this, anyway. Really, the only
reason I'm here is because I need your assistance.

(Two drum beats)

EVE: With her! The whole way that she's dealing with
this, or not dealing with it: sell the house, get rid of his
stuff, don't dwell on the loss, don't take a moment to

grieve, because somehow that's childish, or indulgent; and now she wants to scatter him.

(Drumming)

EVE: Well, I'm sure it's fine, for some people, but my father... It's not what he wanted and it's not what I want.

(Beat)

He used to plant with me, in the garden, up to his elbows in dirt. He would roll it in his fingers, say "this is where life and death are one." He said love and dirt were the only sacred things he knew, but how do you explain that to a woman who never has a hair out of place, who watches you garden from the sunroom? He wanted to be buried, to be part of things that grew, and she is completely dismissing his wishes. And mine. I mean, nowhere in this process have my feelings been acknowledged at all. My need to... to...I don't even know.

What I know is that he doesn't feel dead to me. It feels like she just left him in Kenya.

She was there when he had the heart attack, she was with him. Me, I talked to him on the phone a week before, said, "have a nice time." That was my goodbye to my father.

It doesn't seem like so much to ask, to have a private little burial, something where I don't have to put on a face like at that fucking spectacle of memorial service. Half of me thinks she's just trying to punish me for the tattoo, even though I know that's—

(Three drum beats)

EVE: What, she didn't tell you? I got a tattoo. Which of course she has to make all about her. She sent me this e-mail about how "I won't understand how precious the flesh is until I pass another person though my body." I mean, who says things like that? And you

know it's all about my scar anyway, that was the first
thing out of her mouth, "Why didn't you cover up
your scar—

(Two drum beats)

EVE: Oh, come on. My scar. This one. I know she's told
you.
*(She pulls her sweat jacket down over her shoulder, revealing
a straight white scar on her upper arm.)*
You're kidding, right? I mean this is what sent her into
therapy in the first place. Isn't it?

(Drumming)

EVE: I'm not asking you to break confidentiality, I'm
just asking if she told you about—

(Two drum beats)

EVE: Okay. Okay, well, I'll tell you and if you've heard
it before and you're bored, it'll be your own fault.
Okay, sorry, anyway when I was five years old, my
parents were having this big party. To show off their
new obscenely expensive house. Tons of people. From
the social circle, you know? And I'm trotted out in
this pink dress with a big bow. She wants me to look
presentable, but she pretty much lets me do as I please.
I mingle, you know, 'cause I'm good with adults. Not
so much with children, which is a little inconvenient,
being a child and all, but since I'm the only kid at this
party, I'm kinda in my element. And I'm hanging out
in the back yard because it's dark and late and under
normal circumstances I'd have to be in bed, so I'm
taking advantage of the opportunity, right?
So this guy comes up to me. One of the party-goers. I
don't know him, but that's not weird because I don't
know any of them, really. And he starts talking to me.

*(The tinkle of a few notes on the piano, something sad and
delicate that continues)*

EVE: Well, first I should tell you: there's this statue of a little girl in the yard.

(*The* NAMELESS ONE *appears behind* EVE, *her back to the audience. She still wears the tulle skirt.*)

EVE: It was there when we moved in. She's copper or something, and the rain had created these stains that ran down her face and made it look like she was crying.

(*The* NAMELESS ONE *turns to face us, streaks run down her face.*)

EVE: So, I'm standing by the statue when he comes up to me. Sort of entranced by her, because she's about my size, and she's wearing a dress and bow like I am. And this guy, he says to me, "You know statues were once people, and God thought that they were so perfect that he turned them into stone. But the people don't die," he says. They live forever inside the stone, watching the world go on and on, but never able to speak or run or play, and that's why the little girl is crying… because being a statue isn't any fun.
So, I'm not sure if I believe the guy, but I'm sort of fascinated and disturbed at the same time. Anyway, he's got a drink in his hand—something with ice—and he says, "Do you want to see a trick?"
So I say sure, whatever, 'cause I'm a kid and I like tricks, and I think he's trying to make me feel better after weirding me out with the statue thing.
So he takes a piece of ice out of his glass and he says, "give me your arm,"

(EVE *and the* NAMELESS ONE *hold out their right arms*)

EVE: and he runs this ice cube down my arm and he says, "see that?" And he explains how my arm melted the ice into water.

And I remember thinking, that's not a very good trick.
But then he says, "okay, now I'm going to do it again,
but this time the water's going to be red. But you have
to look at the moon. It'll only work if you look at the
moon."

(EVE *and the* NAMELESS ONE *look at the moon*)

EVE: So I look at the moon and I feel the cold ice on my
arm again, and he says, "now look."

(EVE *and the* NAMELESS ONE *look at their arms.*)

EVE: And there's this stream of red water running
down my arm.
And I was astounded. Astounded.
I looked at him—he was crouched down next to me.
Smiling.

(*The* NAMELESS ONE *smiles at where the man would be.*)

EVE: And I…smiled back at him because, well, because
it was cool. It was a good trick.
And then I heard my mother call me. I dashed across
the yard to show her this red water on my arm before
it disappeared. I figured it would wear off pretty quick,
the way magic does, you know?
And when I ran into the light, someone screamed.
Not her. She was too shocked, too frozen, to scream.
Everyone else was rushing at me, pointing, shouting,
and I was jumping up and down, saying, "It's a trick,
it's a trick!" And when I looked down there was red
water everywhere.

(*A red light from above drenches the* NAMELESS ONE. EVE
is totally lost in this moment.)

EVE: All over my new dress.

(*Light out on the* NAMELESS ONE. *She vanishes.*)

EVE: They said it must have been a razor blade or
a scalpel. They never figured out who he was. If he

was at the party, or some stranger who wandered
in, a neighbor maybe. Everyone was asking me what
happened. When I turned around to point him out, he
was gone....

She's decided it was some vagrant who wandered in, a
predator from outside her world.

But he wasn't a vagrant. He had a tie and a close shave
and a nice smile.

I don't think she really believes it was a vagrant. It just
makes her feel better. To think it wasn't someone she
invited into her home.

I mean, I get why it bothers her. Intellectually, I
understand that I was...violated, I guess, but it never
felt like that. He was just a nice guy sharing some
magic. It didn't even hurt.

But, sometimes I think it cut her to the bone.
When I catch her looking at it, the look on her face....
Then I feel violated.

(Pause, then something occurs to her)

I wonder if he was at Dad's memorial service...the
magic man. That would weird, huh?

(A single drumbeat with the blackout.)

Interlude

(The NAMELESS ONE *enters dancing. She holds several
letters in her hands. One by one she smacks them onto the
floor in time to the music.* REGGIE *enters walking toward
the car. He sees the letters and collects each one. The last
envelope grabs his attention. He straightens up slowly,
looking at the return address. He considers opening it,
then does not. He tosses the letters down in front of the
"passenger seat" of the car and sits in the driver's seat.
Lights fade.)*

Scene 12

(Lights up on the car. REGGIE *is driving,* ATER *is sitting in the passenger seat looking morose, and* DIANE *sits in the back, fidgety and anxious. After a significant silence:)*

DIANE: Is there something wrong with the towels you have?

*(*REGGIE *rolls his eyes in suppressed exasperation.)*

ATER: They are okay. Not big and soft like the ones at the hotel.
I saw DeShawn put some in his bag. I thought it was okay. He did not hide it. He did it in front of everyone. He said it was a "perk".

REGGIE: I think we've been over this enough for one day.

DIANE: I hope they fire him.

ATER: No. He should not lose his job because of me.

DIANE: It's not because of you, it's because he's stealing from his employer.

ATER: But I also stole, and I still have my job.

DIANE: Well, you can thank Deacon Hudson for that. I wasn't getting anywhere with those people.

*(*REGGIE *refrains from responding as he pulls over.)*

REGGIE: All right, Ater. Let's try not to get arrested anymore, okay?

ATER: Yes, Deacon Hudson. Thank you again. Thank you, Diane.

DIANE: Of course, Ater. I'll see you next week.

*(*ATER *gets out of the car and exits.* DIANE *watches him go.)*

DIANE: I'm worried about him. Something's happened. He's behaving…well, I don't know how to describe it, but you see the clothes he's wearing now, and he's so...distant the past few weeks.

(REGGIE *regards* DIANE *through the rearview mirror.*)

REGGIE: He's probably asserting some independence. They tend to cut the apron strings when they get a little more comfortable with their surroundings.

DIANE: But it doesn't feel like that. It seems like he's withdrawing from everyone, even the other Lost Boys. Abraham was teasing him for becoming a homebody and studying all the time, but his grades haven't been very good either.

REGGIE: Well, I'll check on him tomorrow, see how he's doing. All of these boys have survived unimaginable evils. They go through their down periods.

DIANE: I suppose.

REGGIE: Are you going to get in front?

DIANE: What? Oh. My God. Yes. Sorry. Of course.
(She gets into the front seat. She grabs the mail on the floor)
Oh, no. He dropped some letters.

REGGIE: Those are mine.

DIANE: Oh.
(Beat)
Where are you going?

REGGIE: Excuse me?

DIANE: I was just noticing your plane tickets. I'm sorry. I didn't mean to pry.

REGGIE: Those aren't plane tickets.

(DIANE *looks again the envelope again.*)

DIANE: Oh. Sorry. I just assumed. D N A Travel is the same agency I use.

(REGGIE *takes the envelope from* DIANE. *He tears open a corner and looks inside.*)

REGGIE: These are plane tickets.
I don't think I was supposed to open this.

DIANE: No?

REGGIE: I think my wife was trying to surprise me.

DIANE: Oh.

(REGGIE *tucks the letters into an inside coat pocket.*)

REGGIE: I'll figure out how to dig myself out of this later.
Where am I taking you?

DIANE: Oh, you can just drop me at the el.

REGGIE: Well, I'm going back down to the parish, so if you'd like I can drop you at the Red Line near there.

DIANE: That would be fine. Thank you.
(Beat)
Thank you for coming down and talking the hotel people out of pressing charges. And for getting him his job back. I'm not the most clear-headed in those situations. When I saw him in those handcuffs...well, I got a little upset.

REGGIE: So I gathered.

DIANE: You don't like me, do you?

(REGGIE *is so caught off guard that he bursts out laughing.*)

REGGIE: Well, Mrs MacIntyre, you and I don't exactly have a habit of pleasant interactions.

DIANE: Would you say that's entirely my fault?

(Beat)

REGGIE: No.

DIANE: I feel as if you've made some assumptions about me.

REGGIE: Haven't you made assumptions about me?

DIANE: Well, I'm sure I have. I don't know that many black men, to tell you the truth, and absolutely no clergy, so you're really quite outside my comfort zone.

(Three beats)

REGGIE: That's very honest of you.

DIANE: My point is that I'd like us to get along. I've really enjoyed working with Ater, and I feel that we both have his best interests at heart.

REGGIE: Yes.

DIANE: Also, I'm thinking I might apply for the housing coordinator position with the refugee resettlement agency—

REGGIE: Really?

DIANE: Yes. ...My husband died recently, I don't know if Ater told you.

REGGIE: He mentioned it. I'm sorry.

DIANE: Anyhow, I'm feeling the need to...be more occupied. *(Three beats)* I know we've gotten off to a rough start, but I've been out of the work force for so long, and I don't know that many—
If I put you down as a reference, would you say terrible things about me?

(Pause)

REGGIE: I would say that you are passionate about the refugees and a good advocate for them. How's that?

DIANE: That would be very kind of you, Deacon Hudson. *(Beat, she takes a deep breath)* I should tell you, too, that I'm changing my name, well I'm using my maiden name, professionally.

REGGIE: Okay.

DIANE: *(Blathering on a bit)* I'm a little concerned about how it will be perceived. I don't want anyone to think it's some sort of statement about my marriage, because it's not. I loved my husband, I just…
You know, it was always taken for granted that I would take his name. I don't think I realized the significance of it until this minister, this man I hardly knew, was standing there saying, "I now present you with Mr and Mrs Frank MacIntyre". As if, in that moment, I ceased to be.
I guess I have this need to re-Christen myself, now. Unofficially.
I don't know if that makes any sense.

REGGIE: It sounds complicated.

DIANE: Yes.
I even thought about taking my mother's maiden name, or her mother's. It—it's always seemed ridiculous to me that we trace our genealogy through our fathers. Who's to say any of us know who our father really is, the way people behave. Motherhood is much harder to fake.

(Beat)

REGGIE: So what is your maiden name?

(Beat)

DIANE: It's Hudson.

REGGIE: Oh.

(Beat)

DIANE: Does that make you want to kick me out of your car?

(Beat)

REGGIE: Not entirely. *(Pause)* Are you descended from the Winston-Salem Hudsons?

(DIANE *is frozen with shock for a moment.*)

DIANE: Oh, God. Oh God. This is awful.
Your family was…? Really? I mean, I wondered, you always wonder, but I didn't….

REGGIE: My wife's done all the research.

DIANE: Oh God. Could you pull over, please. I'm feeling a little sick.
This is part of what upsets me, you know. About missionaries in Africa. It's more than a little guilt that people like you are walking around with my last name.

REGGIE: Well, I don't think it's quite fair to compare missionaries to slave traders. But you can't shoulder all the responsibility for your ancestors' mistakes.

DIANE: Between the slaves and the hundreds of acres of tobacco they picked, it's not a legacy I'm proud of.

REGGIE: I wasn't asking you to be proud.

(Pause)

DIANE: If you knew your true name. Your African name. Would you take it back?

(Beat)

REGGIE: I don't know that I would.

DIANE: Really?

REGGIE: Having that knowledge—which I will never have—knowing the name of my ancestors, my tribe….
(Pause)
Well, let's just say for argument's sake that I could have it. What does that give me? Do I go back and live among "my people"? Do I deny all that has happened since then? Since Africa. What does a name give me?
But that's in the fairyland of make believe, Diane. Look at my skin. If I could truly trace back and find the name of my fathers, if I could uncover even those

undoubtedly unpleasant secrets,don't you think I
would end up at a man with the last name Hudson? Or
Jackson or Williams or Washington? Taking an African
name would be a form of denial that I'm not capable
of. Now, maybe you, changing your name, maybe
that's not denial. I don't know you and I don't want to
judge. But I know for me, it would be.

(Pause)

DIANE: I'm sorry.

REGGIE: I appreciate the apology.
(He is suddenly amused.)

DIANE: What?

REGGIE: I just think it's funny.
That you.
Ms Diane MacIntyre Hudson whatever your name is…
you are probably the cream in my coffee.

(REGGIE laughs as the lights shift.)

Interlude

*(African pop music plays loudly. EVE and the NAMELESS
ONE enter dancing to the music. EVE wears subdued
clubbing clothes. Though EVE never seems to see the
NAMELESS ONE she is guiding her through the dance.
ATER enters and heads toward the sofa of his apartment.
The NAMELESS ONE intercepts him, trying to engage him
in the dance. ATER avoids her, stepping back and around,
sitting on the sofa. DIANE has also entered and set down
a half-empty wine bottle. She sits on the sofa oblivious to
everything. The NAMELESS ONE sniffs the wine, a little
concerned by its contents. She turns to find EVE in the midst
of a spastic dance riff. The NAMELESS ONE rushes back to
EVE, calming and redirecting her movement. EVE dances
off.)*

Scene 13

(Lights up on ATER's *apartment. He and* DIANE *sit on opposite sides of the sofa watching T V. A bottle of wine sits by* DIANE, *she is drinking out of a juice glass. The* NAMELESS ONE *sits nearby looking uncomfortable. The lights are fairly dim and the T V flickers on their faces. It is late.* DIANE *turns off the T V.)*

DIANE: Well, that was disappointing. Everyone said it was so good.

(Bringing her glass to the kitchen)

Do you want me to leave the rest of the wine?

ATER: No. You should take it.

*(*DIANE *corks the wine.)*

DIANE: You needn't act like such a teetotaler, Ater. I've seen the empty beer cans in your garbage, which you should be recycling, by the way.

ATER: The elders told us, before we left Kakuma, that we should stay away from white girls and alcohol.

DIANE: So, I'm corrupting you with my Napa Valley Pinot Noir, am I?

*(*ATER *does not answer, does not look at* DIANE.)

DIANE: Ater? Are you all right?

ATER: I do not understand why we do this.

DIANE: Do what?

ATER: See this movie. I do not see the lesson.

DIANE: I— Well... There is no lesson. I thought it might be nice to spend the evening together. As friends.

ATER: I do not see you this way.

(Beat)

DIANE: Oh.

ATER: If you were Dinka, you would be friends with my mother, and I would know you and I would be polite, but we would not watch a movie together.

DIANE: I see.
Well, I didn't mean to make you uncomfortable.
I've just been worried about you. You haven't seemed yourself lately. I thought, maybe...you needed someone to talk to.

ATER: I am fine.

DIANE: If you want to go see Doctor Mazur again/ I would be happy to—

ATER: /No.

(Pause)

DIANE: All right. I guess I should go then.

(When ATER *does not respond,* DIANE *begins to gather up her things. She spies a letter peeking out from a sofa cushion.)*

DIANE: Oh, you're about to lose a letter here. I hope it's not a bill.

*(*ATER *takes it from* DIANE.*)*

ATER: It's mine.

(There is a knock at the door. DIANE *answers it. It is* EVE. *She holds a shopping bag in one hand.)*

EVE: Hey—

DIANE: Eve.

EVE: Mom.

DIANE & EVE: What are you doing here?

DIANE: Is something wrong?

EVE: What? No. I was just coming to see Ater.

DIANE: Oh. Well…I guess I was just leaving. Goodnight, Ater.

(ATER *looks at the letter, unmoving. The* NAMELESS ONE *sits near him, concerned.*)

DIANE: Goodnight dear.

(DIANE *walks past* EVE *and exits.*)

(EVE *enters the apartment and closes the door. The* NAMELESS ONE *beckons her, and she comes, though she does not see.*)

EVE: Hi.

ATER: Hello, Eve. Did you have fun dancing?

EVE: Yeah, we had a great time. It's nice to have some male friends who actually like to dance.
(*Beat*)
Everyone is down the hall at Jok's if you want to come have a beer or something.

ATER: No. Thank you.

EVE: What was my mother doing here?

ATER: I do not know, exactly.

EVE: Yeah. (*Beat*) Well, I'll tell you why I'm here: I brought you a present.

(EVE *pulls Brutus the teddy bear out of the bag and sets him on the sofa. The* NAMELESS ONE *touches the bear fondly.*)

EVE: I even washed him.

ATER: (*Picking him up*) This is Brutus.

EVE: Yeah.

ATER: You are giving me your friend?

EVE: Well, yeah, see, after you were at the house…it occurred to me that you probably don't have a single thing that belonged to your father, nothing he gave

you, nothing he wore…. I mean, your whole village
was burned, right?

(The NAMELESS ONE *moves to* ATER.*)*

EVE: And there I was sifting through an entire house
full of possessions, trying to figure out what has
meaning….

(Pause. She tries to contain her emotions.)

You know, when I was a girl, studying history in
school—Western history, because that's all they taught
us—I remember being so grateful that I wasn't living
through terrible times. But the thing is, I was living
through terrible times. I just didn't know about them
and they weren't happening to me.

(As she wipes her face.)

Anyhow, maybe Brutus will help you sleep. I don't
know that he wards off evil spirits or anything, but
he's really soothing, especially if lay your head on him
right here. And it's not like I sleep with him anymore—
his talents are totally wasted on me.

So I hope you'll take him.

ATER: Thank you, Eve. This is very kind.
(He sets Brutus down next to him.)

EVE: Are you sure you don't want to go to Jok's?

ATER: No. I do not think I will go.

*(*ATER *turns the letter over in his hand.* EVE *watches him a
moment.)*

EVE: What's that?

ATER: It's a letter from the Red Cross.

(The NAMELESS ONE *returns a steadying hand to* ATER's
shoulder.)

EVE: What do they want?

ATER: They write to tell me that my mother is alive and living in a camp in northern Uganda.

EVE: Oh.

My God.

Really?

ATER: Yes. My sisters are alive, also. And one brother.

(Beat)

EVE: Ater. That's incredible.

ATER: Yes.

EVE: You got this letter today?

ATER: Last month.

(Beat)

EVE: Last month?

ATER: I have an appointment to talk to my mother tomorrow. I have not spoken to her in fourteen years.

(Pause)

EVE: You must be kinda nervous, huh? I mean, I would be.

ATER: I will have to tell her about Lual—my younger brother—that I was too weak to carry him and he died. That I could not bury him.

(Pause)

EVE: I'm sure she won't blame you.

ATER: I will have to tell her that we left him under a bush with a cross of stones over his body. And she will know, like I do, that the animals must have eaten him. And then she will tell me that my father and my second oldest brother are dead. I know this because it says so in the letter, but she will tell me anyway. And she will probably ask me to send money like Abraham

does for his mother. And she will tell me that things
are still very bad in Sudan.

(Pause)

EVE: But you...you already knew that your father was
dead, right?

ATER: Yes. I thought I knew this.

EVE: Mom said you saw the Arab guys, the
Northerners, shoot him.

ATER: I heard the shot. Many shots. I saw him lying
on the ground. I heard the blood in his throat when he
called my name. ...But it does not feel like I know these
things when I read his death in the letter. I did not
know I had been holding hope for him in my heart.

*(As the lights fade, ATER places the letter back under his
pillow.)*

Scene 14

*(Lights up on DIANE at the shrink's office and on ATER
sitting in a separate space in a solitary chair with a phone
up to his ear. When he speaks there is a faint echo of his
words like the feedback you often hear on a long distance
conversation.)*

ATER: Ee keda maa? Ee keda?
(Hello, Mother? Hello?)

(Drumming)

DIANE: I haven't decided.

ATER: Ee qen maa, Ee qen Ater. Ee. Keda?
(Yes, it is me Mother, it is Ater. Yes. Hello.)

DIANE: I don't want another empty Christian ceremony
that means nothing to me.

(Drumming)

ATER: Qen atou Amerika, pan col Cicago.
(Yes I am in America, in Chicago.)

DIANE: Eve is fine. I mean, she's angry that her father is gone, taking it out on me.

ATER: Piny aliir apei etene.
(It is very cold here.)

(Drumming)

DIANE: She did?

(Drumming)

ATER: Qen areer kek miith Muonyjieng Qonditic.
(I am living with other Dinka in a large apartment.)

DIANE: So I should pretend for her sake? Buy a headstone, be a hypocrite?

ATER: Qen eela Pan eebun ku Qen ee luoi.
(I am going to school and I have a job.)

(Drumming)

DIANE: Well, that's an easy thing to say, Ben, but making up my own rules is not something I've ever been adept at.

ATER: Maa / / / / Awic ba yii lek thong Lual.
(Mother…I must tell you about Lual.)

(Lights change)

Interlude

(Drums thunder. The NAMELESS ONE enters with spear and shield. ATER, despondent from his phone call, hears the drums. The NAMELESS ONE comes up beside him doing a warrior dance. She hands him the shield and he takes up the dance as well. The music intensifies as the dance peaks. ATER lets out a battle cry. Black out)

Scene 15

(In the darkness a pounding on the door)

DIANE: *(Off stage)* Ater, just open the door.

ATER: No.

REGGIE: *(Off stage)* Ater, the police are allowing me talk to you first, but their patience is limited.

ATER: They are outside?

REGGIE: *(Off stage)* They're downstairs.

ATER: Will they arrest me?

DIANE: *(Off stage)* They just need to ask you what happened.

ATER: They will put me in jail.

DIANE: *(Off stage)* Ater, they know you were defending yourself.

REGGIE: *(O S. Booming)* Ater, OPEN THIS DOOR.

(Lights up as ATER unlocks the door and retreats. He holds a bloody rag on his arm. REGGIE and DIANE rush in at him. The NAMELESS ONE, holding the spear and shield stands aside.)

DIANE: Ater, you have Abraham worried sick.
Let me see your arm.
I need a new towel. Keep pressure on it.

REGGIE: *(Overlapping with DIANE)* Are you—you're bleeding.
Is this the only place he stabbed you?
How did this happen, Ater?

(DIANE goes to the bathroom.)

ATER: Deshawn is angry about losing his job. He jumped on me when I left the hotel. I felt a pain in my arm. I don't remember what happened then.

REGGIE: Ater, you put the boy in the hospital, how can you not remember?

ATER: He is not dead?

REGGIE: He's in bad shape, but he's not dead.

ATER: *(Surprised, without malice)* I meant to kill him.

DIANE: *(Whispering)* Ater! How can you say that? Don't you dare say that to the police.

ATER: I did not know who he was or where I was, if I was at Kakuma or if I was still a boy. I thought, I will kill him so he will not kill me, and then I was running. Running until I got here.
I'm glad he is not dead. He is not worth killing. He is not a warrior. Only a stupid towel-thief.

REGGIE: Ater, you shouldn't talk like that.

DIANE: I think a doctor should look at this.

ATER: *(Pulling away)* Let it bleed.

DIANE: It might scar.

ATER: It does not matter!

(The NAMELESS ONE *points the spear at* REGGIE *in warning.)*

REGGIE: Ater, you need to calm down before you talk to the police.

ATER: I do not like it here!
(Angry)
I do not like being inside all the time. I don't like the pavement and the smell of the buses. I want to go back to Africa, go back to the life I was supposed to have. Everything here is too loud and complicated. I just want to be home. Some place where I do not have to wear all these clothes, where I can stand with my herd of cows and sing them songs. But I cannot even do that because there are no cows for me.

REGGIE: I know it's hard, Ater.

ATER: You do not know! You do not know anything I am feeling. You do not know what it is to fight for your life and your home, to not be able to fight because you have been moved across an ocean.

(Slowly he buries his emotions.)

I try to be grateful that I can come to America, have a place to live, food to eat, school, opportunity…but I want to go back. We are not lost little boys. We are not your children. We are warriors who have been taken from our war in the name of kindness and charity. Who will fight for our land while I fold towels and go to school? There is no place for our people.

REGGIE: There's a place for you here, Ater.

ATER: It is not the same. It is not our home. My freedom here is small and painful if my family cannot be free.

…I wish I did not remember how it was when I was a baby. I wish my family was dead. Then, maybe, if I had nothing left to care about, I could become an American.

(Lights change.)

Interlude

(The NAMELESS ONE appears with REGGIE's robes. She dresses him. She hangs African beads around his neck. Organ music and voices singing a hymn. ATER and EVE sit in a front "pew" as REGGIE takes his place behind the pulpit. Lights change.)

Scene 16

(As REGGIE *finishes his sermon, the fractured, colored light of stained glass windows falls on the audience.)*

REGGIE: …which is why we must always remember how God has blessed us in our lives.
(Pause)
Before you go on with your day, I wanted to tell you that I'll be gone for a few Sundays next month. My dear wife Lorraine has surprised me with a vacation, a trip to Africa. Tanzania.
(Beat)
I'll be honest with you: I have mixed feelings about the trip. Part of me is filled with that adrenaline-soaked anticipation that comes from knowing I'm about to embark on an adventure. Part of me is afraid. Afraid of being in a plane for so long. Flying over the ocean. And then there is the guilt: The piece of me that doesn't feel like I deserve this indulgence because I know that the longing to travel back to Africa is much more urgent and painful for my Sudanese friends who sit with us here today.
(He glances at ATER.*)*
And then there is this vague sense of uncertainty. The day the plane tickets arrived in the mail…. I thought it was something else in this non-descript business envelope. I thought it was a bit of false comfort that I had foolishly sent away for. A piece of paper that would try to tell me who I am, where I'm from, and where I belong. I didn't trust this piece of paper, but I thought it might change me somehow, and that's a scary thing. To think some tree pulp will change how you feel about yourself.
When I realized what it was, where we were going, I pulled out the passport that my optimistic Lorraine had made me get several years ago. And it struck me

as odd, as I stood there looking at it, that it is the only
piece of paper I possess that claims me as a citizen
of this country. This little blue book. It says I am an
American, which is not something I think of a lot.
We're a strange breed, Americans. For some reason
we cling to the place that our people came from, no
matter how many generations ago we emigrated…or
were brought here. You ask a man about his ethnicity,
he will say he's Polish, German, Lithuanian, even if
he has never set foot in Europe. He will not say he is
American. I don't know that I've ever said the words.
I am American. They feel strange in my mouth, and
slightly untrue. Perhaps one must leave home to
feel the truth in these words. Perhaps when I am in
Tanzania I will know what it is to feel American and
not have it be merely a book in my pocket that I dare
not lose.
The day after the tickets arrived, after I had my little
passport epiphany, the other envelope came.
The one I was expecting. The one I had been dreading.
But now I understood that this trip was going to tell
me more about myself than any information this letter
might hold. So I burned it without opening it. A violent
act, I realize, but to tear it up, to toss it away was not
enough.
My point is that I am uncertain of my place in this
world. I don't know where I came from, and I realize
that this journey to Africa may leave me with more
questions than answers. I don't want to fool myself
into thinking that I will get there and feel like I belong.
But there is one thing I do know. I belong to this
church, to God, and to all of you. And it is the one
thing I do not need a piece of paper for.
I know that some of you out there feel that you don't
belong. Either at work or at home or maybe even in
this church, this country. But I ask you today, as you

leave this house of God, to look in the eyes of at least one stranger and know that they belong to you and you to them, just a tiny bit, because you both sat here and celebrated this Mass with me.

(Lights fade.)

Interlude

(As the church scene fades and transitions, the NAMELESS ONE *hands* EVE *a letter. She opens it as she walks into the* MACINTYRE *house space. She reads it, folds it, puts it in her pocket and sits on the floor. The* NAMELESS ONE *places the box of ashes in* EVE's *lap.)*

Scene 17

(Lights up on the MacIntyre house. The walls are bare except for the shield and spear. EVE *sits in a warm spot of sunlight on the floor. The* NAMELESS ONE *can be seen in the garden, posing as the statue.)*

DIANE: *(Off stage)* Did you call the club, make sure that the nursery delivered the tree?

EVE: Yes, Mom, it's there.

DIANE: Did you check your nook in the attic?

EVE: I checked everything. *(To the box)* God, this is sad. I think the house is sad.

DIANE: *(Offstage)* So Ater seemed all right?

EVE: Well, you know, it's kind of hard to tell. There isn't any nerve damage in his arm, at least.

DIANE: *(Entering)* Is he still refusing to sign a complaint against DeShawn?

EVE: Yeah. He says he doesn't want to hurt DeShawn's chances of getting another job.

DIANE: I really don't understand these boys.

EVE: Sometimes I wonder if this is the first head he's bashed in.

DIANE: Eve! How can you say that?

EVE: I don't mean it in a judgmental way, but come on, Mom, he did survive a civil war...somehow.

DIANE: I need your keys.

(EVE *stares at* DIANE *for a beat, then pulls out a mess of keys begins to disconnect her house keys.*)

EVE: I'm going to miss this house.

DIANE: I'm not.

EVE: That's not true.

DIANE: I never felt safe here.

(Beat)

EVE: I did.

DIANE: Really?

EVE: Yeah.

DIANE: I never felt like you were safe.

EVE: I know. A different house wouldn't have changed that.

(Beat)

DIANE: That's what your father always said.

(EVE *hands* DIANE *the keys.* DIANE *tosses them in her bag and takes the spear and shield off the wall.*)

EVE: I got accepted to a field internship in Ecuador.

(Beat)

DIANE: Really?

EVE: Yeah. I leave in June.

(Beat)

DIANE: Congratulations.

(Though ATER's *apartment is not lit, he enters with some school books and sits on the sofa with Brutus, doing some homework. Lights do not come up on him.)*

EVE: You're not going to unravel on me?

DIANE: Would you like me to?

EVE: No.

(Beat)

DIANE: Is there anything else you need to say goodbye to? The shrubbery?

EVE: I already said goodbye to the shrubbery.

DIANE: I guess we're ready, then.

EVE: I guess so.

*(*DIANE *and* EVE *both take a last look at the house.* EVE *looks out the window in the fourth wall.)*

EVE: I'm going to miss the statue.

DIANE: Me too.

EVE: *(Quietly)* She knows all my secrets.

*(*DIANE strokes EVE's hair. EVE does not object.

DIANE: Remember how you used to tell me that statues were people frozen by God? That's what she's like.

EVE: Yeah.

DIANE: Where did you ever get that idea?

(Beat)

EVE: I don't remember.

DIANE: Well, we should go.

*(*DIANE *takes the spear and shield off the wall.)*

DIANE: Do you mind if I drive?

EVE: …No?

(ATER *rises and goes to the door, closing it as the lights crossfade to* ATER's *apartment.*)

(ATER *closes the door.* DIANE *stands awkwardly with the shield.*)

ATER: Hello, Diane.

DIANE: Hello, Ater.

ATER: You have not been to see me in many weeks.

DIANE: I know. I'm sorry. I've been busy with my new job, and…well, to tell you the truth…
I'm not sure where I fit into your life anymore. You don't need a volunteer now, and clearly I'm not the best liaison for your scrapes with the law….

(ATER *and* DIANE *share a smile.*)

ATER: You should come to Thursday night dinners at Saint Bartholomew's. We are always there.

DIANE: Maybe I'll do that.

ATER: Why do you have that shield?

DIANE: Oh, I brought it for you. The dealer said it was Dinka. I hope that's true.

ATER: I am…not the right person to ask. I have not seen a Dinka shield since I was a boy.

DIANE: Well, I thought you might like to have a little piece of home. Even if you don't remember it.

ATER: I think maybe I cannot accept this. Eve said it is worth a lot of money.

DIANE: Yes, it is worth a lot of money. If you ever wanted to sell it, I'd be happy to put you in touch with the dealer.

ATER: Why would I sell your gift?

DIANE: I don't know. Maybe to visit your family someday. See your mother. Eve said you've been in touch with her.

ATER: Yes.

DIANE: I know how badly she must want to see you.

(ATER *nods, unsure what to make of this.*)

DIANE: Well, we should go. Eve's waiting in the car.

ATER: Am I dressed okay?

DIANE: Yes.

(ATER *sets the shield down on the sofa next to Brutus as the lights change. The* NAMELESS ONE *walks downstage center and ritualistically spreads dirt on the ground around her feet.* ATER, DIANE, *and* EVE *walk towards her with reverence.* EVE *sprinkles some of the ashes with the dirt as* ATER *and* DIANE *look on. The* NAMELESS ONE *holds her arms up like branches. As the lights change* ATER *looks up at the sky.*)

ATER: The stars are coming out.
I have not seen them since I left Africa.

DIANE: Really?

ATER: I thought maybe there were no stars here, but Deacon Hudson said they were hidden behind all the light of Chicago.

EVE: Yeah.

ATER: I have missed them.

(DIANE *and* EVE *watch* ATER *search the sky.*)

ATER: When we were going to Ethiopia, we mostly walked at night, letting the sky guide us. (*Turning back to* DIANE *and* EVE) I'm sorry.
I did not mean to disrupt the ceremony.

EVE: You didn't.

ATER: Is it usual in America to bury the father with a tree?

EVE: No.

DIANE: Since the club wanted to plant a tree in Frank's memory and we weren't sure what to do with the ashes, well, we thought it would be nice.

ATER: It was a beautiful sacrament to witness. It made me think of many people.
Thank you…for sharing it with me.

DIANE: Of course.

EVE: Do you want to do the last bit yourself, Mom?

(After a moment's deliberation, DIANE kneels down, spills the last bit of ash onto the ground and pushes the dirt around the "tree" with her hands. She runs some through her fingers.)

DIANE: It's like velvet.

EVE: Yeah.

ATER: I don't know these patterns. These are not my stars.

EVE: *(Rising)* Oh, well, some of them, but…yeah. They're not all the same stars…this far North.

(As DIANE stands she loses her balance, and reaches for a tree branch to stabilize herself. The "tree" reaches back and finally she sees the NAMELESS ONE for the first time.)

ATER: I have left everything behind.

(EVE slips her hand into ATER's, for comfort, as the NAMELESS ONE wipes a tear from DIANE's face and shows it to her. Lights fade.)

END OF PLAY

END OF TEXT

www.ingramcontent.com/pod-product-compliance
Lightning Source LLC
Chambersburg PA
CBHW052139090426
42741CB00009B/2149